哈佛蓝星双语

Today's Most Popular Study Guides

百年孤独
One Hundred Years of Solitude

〔哥〕Gabriel Garcia Marquez　原著
Margaret Miller　导读
Josh Perry
杜晓轩　翻译
苏伶童　校对
张滨江　主审

SMARTER　*BETTER*　*FASTER*

天津科技翻译出版公司

著作权合同登记号:图字:02—2007—95

图书在版编目(CIP)数据

百年孤独:英汉对照/(哥伦比亚)马尔克斯(Marquez,G.G.)著;杜晓轩译. 2版. —天津:天津科技翻译出版公司,2008.1 (2009.1重印)
(哈佛蓝星双语名著导读)
书名原文:One Hundred Years of Solitude
ISBN 978-7-5433-2285-1

Ⅰ.百… Ⅱ.①马…②杜… Ⅲ.①英语-汉语-对照读物②长篇小说-哥伦比亚-现代 Ⅳ.H319.4:I

中国版本图书馆 CIP 数据核字(2007)第 163188 号

One Hundred Years of Solitude By Marquez, G. G.
Copyright © 2002 by SparkNotes LLC
All rights reserved.
Chinese edition © 2008 by Tianjin Science & Technology Translation & Publishing Co.
This Chinese edition was published by arrangement with Sterling Publishing., Inc., 387 Park Avenue South. New York, NY 10016.

哈佛蓝星双语名著导读:百年孤独
TODAY'S MOST POPULAR STUDY GUIDES

出　　版	天津科技翻译出版公司
出 版 人	蔡　颢
地　　址	天津市南开区白堤路 244 号
邮政编码	300192
电　　话	022-87894896
传　　真	022-87895650
网　　址	www.tsttpc.com
印　　刷	高等教育出版社印刷厂
发　　行	全国新华书店

版本记录:846×1092　32 开本　6.125 印张　123 千字
　　　　　2009 年 1 月第 2 版　2009 年 1 月第 3 次印刷
　　　　　定价:10.00 元

版权所有·侵权必究
(如有印装问题,可与出版社调换)

CONTENTS 目录

CONTEXT ··· 2
来龙·去脉

PLOT OVERVIEW ······································ 8
情节·览

CHARACTER LIST ···································· 14
角色·亮相

   A Note about the Names　名字注释 ············ 14

   The Buendia Family　布恩地亚家族 ············· 16

      First Generation　第一代 ······················ 16

      Second Generation　第二代 ·················· 18

      Third Generation　第三代 ····················· 22

      Fourth Generation　第四代 ···················· 24

      Fifth Generation　第五代 ······················ 26

      Sixth Generation　第六代 ····················· 30

   Characters Who Are Not Members of the Buendia Family ··· 30
   非布恩地亚家族成员角色

ANALYSIS OF MAJOR CHARACT ················ 36
主角·赏

   Jose Arcadio Buendia　霍塞·阿卡迪奥·布恩地亚 ··· 36

   Colonel Aureliano Buendia　奥雷良诺·布恩地亚上校 ··· 38

   Ursula Iguaran　乌苏拉·伊瓜兰 ·················· 40

   Aureliano (II)　奥雷良诺第二 ····················· 42

THEMES, MOTIFS & SYMBOLS ··················· 45
主题·主题成分·象征

   The Subjectivity of Experienced Reality ············ 45
   现实经历的主观性

   The Inseparability of Past, Present, and Future ········ 46
   过去、现在和将来的不可分离性

The Power of Reading and of Language		46
阅读和语言的魔力		
Memory and Forgetfulness 记忆和忘记		50
The Bible 圣经		50
The Gypsies 吉普赛人		52
Little Gold Fishes 小金鱼		52
The Railroad 铁路		54
The English Encyclopedia 大英百科全书		56
The Golden Chamber Pot 金便盆		56

SUMMARY & ANALYSIS 58
断章·取义

Chapter 1 – 2	第1~2章	58
Chapter 3 – 4	第3~4章	70
Chapter 5 – 6	第5~6章	80
Chapter 7 – 9	第7~9章	90
Chapter 10 – 11	第10~11章	102
Chapter 12 – 13	第12~13章	114
Chapter 14 – 15	第14~15章	124
Chapter 16 – 17	第16~17章	134
Chapter 18 – 20	第18~20章	142

IMPORTANT QUOTATIONS EXPLAINED 154
语出·有因

KEY FACTS 164
作品档案

STUDY QUESTIONS & ESSAY TOPICS 172
问题·论题

REVIEW & RESOURCES 182
回味·深入

Quiz 四选一	182
Suggestions for Further Reading 相关链接	188

致读者

亲爱的读者,在这个多元文化的世界里,渴望知识、钟情文学、热爱英语的你是否希望站在巨人的肩膀上摘星呢?

"哈佛蓝星双语名著导读"系列是全美最风行的经典名著导读笔记,由哈佛学生们融会名著阅读和文学学习精华,亲笔撰写而成。蓝星系列精选了来自世界各国的杰出经典著作,以经典性和流行性并重的名著为素材,以明晰的风格和地道的语言,解读名著精华和具有时代性的主题和思想。每一分册都包括名著的创作背景、人物分析、主题解析、篇章讲解、重要引文释义、作品档案,并且附有相关的思考题、推荐论题、小测验以及延伸阅读篇目。

如今"蓝星"漂洋过海,轻轻落在了国内英语学习读者的掌中,读者不需走出国门,即可轻松掌握哈佛课堂上的知识。蓝星系列丰富的内容编排,使我们不仅仅停留于名著内容的了解,而且对著作的精华和内涵有更全面、深入的掌握,进而对英语语言和文化做更进一步的了解和研究。蓝星精辟、明晰的编写风格让"半天阅读一本名著"成为现实,使我们在有限的闲暇时间内阅读更多的书,同时迅速增强英语水平,提高文学修养,增加谈资。

天津科技翻译出版公司之前推出的"蓝星"系列50册,在图书市场上收到了很好的反响。本次新推出的品种同样精挑细选了国外近现代经典作品,以期进一步丰富该系列的内容。本次出版仍由天津外国语学院张滨江教授和青年教师负责翻译和审校,并严格按照原作的风格,提供原汁原味的英语环境,让读者自由地阅读、想象和发挥。

蓝星闪耀,伴你前行!

CONTEXT

Gabriel García Márquez was born in 1928, in the small town of Aracataca, Colombia. He started his career as a journalist, first publishing his short stories and novels in the mid-1950s. When *One Hundred Years of Solitude* was published in his native Spanish in 1967, as Cien años de soledad, García Márquez achieved true international fame; he went on to receive the Nobel Prize for Literature in 1982. Still a prolific writer of fiction and journalism, García Márquez was perhaps the central figure in the so-called Latin Boom, which designates the rise in popularity of Latin-American writing in the 1960s and 1970s. *One Hundred Years of Solitude* is perhaps the most important, and the most widely read, text to emerge from that period. It is also a central and pioneering work in the movement that has become known as magical realism, which was characterized by the dreamlike and fantastic elements woven into the fabric of its fiction.

In part, the magic of García Márquez's writing is a result of his rendering the world through a child's eyes: he has said that nothing really important has happened to him since he was eight years old and that the atmosphere of his books is the atmosphere of childhood. García Márquez's native town of Aracataca is the inspiration for much of his fiction, and readers of *One Hundred Years of Solitude* may recognize many parallels between the real-life history of García Márquez's hometown and the history of the fictional town of Macondo.

来龙·去脉

加夫列尔·加西亚·马尔克斯于1928年出生在哥伦比亚小镇阿拉卡塔卡。他以记者身份开始职业生涯,在20世纪50年代中期陆续发表了他的短篇和长篇小说。1967年,当《百年孤独》以他的母语西班牙语发表时,加西亚·马尔克斯获得了真正的国际声誉,并于1982年获得诺贝尔文学奖。在标志着拉美文学流行崛起的20世纪60年代至70年代,即所谓拉美文学"爆炸"时期,作为小说和新闻业界的多产作家,加西亚·马尔克斯被誉为"爆炸"中的核心角色。而《百年孤独》这部小说也许是这一时期最重要而且最流行的作品。该小说还被誉为魔幻现实主义运动中的核心和先驱作品。魔幻现实主义融合了梦幻和幻想的成分,是以虚构为特征的创作手法。

加西亚·马尔克斯以一个儿童的视角呈现他所想要表现的世界,从某种程度上说,这一点增添了他创作的魅力。他曾经这么说,对于他来说,自从8岁以后,再也没有任何真正重要的事情发生在他身上了;他的创作背景基于他童年时期的现实经历。加西亚·马尔克斯从他出生的小镇阿拉卡塔卡获得了他大部分创作的灵感,《百年孤独》的读者可以在加西亚·马尔克斯家乡现实生活的历史与小说中虚构的马贡多小镇的历史之间发现许多类似之处。现实中的家乡小镇和小说中的小镇上,都是在20世纪初外国水果公

In both towns, foreign fruit companies brought many prosperous plantations to nearby locations at the beginning of the twentieth century. By the time of García Márquez's birth, however, Aracataca had begun a long, slow decline into poverty and obscurity, a decline mirrored by the fall of Macondo in *One Hundred Years of Solitude.*

Even as it draws from García Márquez's provincial experiences, *One Hundred Years of Solitude* also reflects political ideas that apply to Latin America as a whole. Latin America once had a thriving population of native Aztecs and Incas, but, slowly, as European explorers arrived, the native population had to adjust to the technology and capitalism that the outsiders brought with them. Similarly, Macondo begins as a very simple settlement, and money and technology become common only when people from the outside world begin to arrive. In addition to mirroring this early virginal stage of Latin America's growth, *One Hundred Years of Solitude* reflects the current political status of various Latin American countries. Just as Macondo undergoes frequent changes in government, Latin American nations, too, seem unable to produce governments that are both stable and organized. The various dictatorships that come into power throughout the course of *One Hundred Years of Solitude*, for example, mirror dictatorships that have ruled in Nicaragua, Panama, and Cuba. García Márquez's real-life political leanings are decidedly revolutionary: he is a friend of Fidel Castro. But his depictions of cruel dictatorships show that his revolutionary sympathies do not extend to the cruel governments that revolutionary party sometimes produces.

司带来了水果种植的繁荣。在加西亚·马尔克斯出生的时期，阿拉卡塔卡小镇逐渐开始衰败，变成了一个穷乡僻壤。在《百年孤独》小说中，虚构小镇马贡多的毁灭则映射了现实生活中阿拉卡塔卡小镇的衰败。

尽管《百年孤独》的创作基于加西亚·马尔克斯个人的现实经历，但是小说仍然反映了整个拉丁美洲的政治思想。拉丁美洲曾经孕育了本土繁荣的阿兹台克和印加文明。但是随着欧洲探险者逐渐登上这片土地，土著居民不得不开始适应外来入侵者给他们带来的现代化技术和资本主义。同样，马贡多在创建的初期只是一个淳朴的小镇，但是随着外部世界的入侵，资本和技术变成了人们普遍接受的事物。除了反映拉丁美洲早期的原始发展阶段之外，《百年孤独》还折射了拉美不同国家的政治现状。同马贡多频繁的政权更迭一样，现实中的拉美国家同样无法建立既稳定又有序的政府。例如，在《百年孤独》的历史演变过程中，小说通过描写马贡多专制政权的频繁更迭来影射尼加拉瓜、巴拿马和古巴这些国家的独裁统治。在现实生活中，加西亚·马尔克斯在政治上的态度明显倾向于革命主义：他是菲德勒·卡斯特罗的朋友。但是他在小说中对残酷政权的刻画说明他虽然对革命主义抱有同情，但并没有怜悯革命主义专制的统治。

One Hundred Years of Solitude, then, is partly an attempt to render the reality of García Márquez's own experiences in a fictional narrative. Its importance, however, can also be traced back to the way it appeals to broader spheres of experience. *One Hundred Years of Solitude* is an extremely ambitious novel. To a certain extent, in its sketching of the histories of civil war, plantations, and labor unrest, *One Hundred Years of Solitude* tells a story about Colombian history and, even more broadly, about Latin America's struggles with colonialism and with its own emergence into modernity. García Márquez's masterpiece, however, appeals not just to Latin American experiences, but to larger questions about human nature. It is, in the end, a novel as much about specific social and historical circumstances—disguised by fiction and fantasy—as about the possibility of love and the sadness of alienation and solitude.

《百年孤独》在某种程度上试图通过虚构的故事来再现加西亚·马尔克斯个人的现实经历。但是它的重要性还在于它以这种再现方式折射了更加广阔范围内的社会现实。《百年孤独》是一部非同凡响的小说，一定程度上说，《百年孤独》小说通过描写内战历史、种植园以及劳工骚乱讲述了一部哥伦比亚史，甚至从更广泛的层次上说，是讲述一部有关拉丁美洲与殖民主义之间的斗争史以及拉丁美洲向现代化发展的历史。加西亚·马尔克斯的这部宏篇巨著不仅反映了拉丁美洲的社会现实，而且在更深层次上折射了有关人性的问题。总之，这既是一部在虚构和幻想掩饰下，反映特定社会和历史现实的小说，又是一部关于现实的爱和产生于异化与隔绝的悲哀的小说。

PLOT OVERVIEW

One Hundred Years of Solitude is the history of the isolated town of Macondo and of the family who founds it, the Buendías. For years, the town has no contact with the outside world, except for gypsies who occasionally visit, peddling technologies like ice and telescopes. The patriarch of the family, José Arcadio Buendía, is impulsive and inquisitive. He remains a leader who is also deeply solitary, alienating himself from other men in his obsessive investigations into mysterious matters. These character traits are inherited by his descendents throughout the novel. His older child, José Arcadio, inherits his vast physical strength and his impetuousness. His younger child, Aureliano, inherits his intense, enigmatic focus. Gradually, the village loses its innocent, solitary state when it establishes contact with other towns in the region. Civil wars begin, bringing violence and death to peaceful Macondo, which, previously, had experienced neither, and Aureliano becomes the leader of the Liberal rebels, achieving fame as Colonel Aureliano Buendía. Macondo changes from an idyllic, magical, and sheltered place to a town irrevocably connected to the outside world through the notoriety of Colonel Buendía. Macondo's governments change several times during and after the war. At one point, Arcadio, the cruelest of the Buendías, rules dictatorially and is eventually shot by a firing squad. Later, a mayor is appointed,

情节·览

《百年孤独》讲述了一个与世隔绝的小镇——马贡多及其创建者布恩地亚家族的历史。除了偶尔前来兜售诸如制冰以及望远镜技术的吉普赛人外,马贡多小镇几乎与外界没有任何来往。霍塞·阿卡迪奥·布恩地亚是家族首领,他性格冲动、好奇心强。虽然身为家族的首领,但是他陷入了不能自拔的孤独之中,把自己与外界隔绝起来,沉迷于对神秘事物的探索。在小说中,他的性格特征被他的后代们继承了下来。长子霍塞·阿卡迪奥继承了他高大壮硕的身材以及鲁莽、冲动的性格。二儿子奥雷良诺沿袭了他执着、难以琢磨的神秘特征。自从与周边的小镇有了来往之后,马贡多小镇逐渐失去了它的纯朴,它与世隔绝的状态也被打破了。内战的爆发给这个平静的小镇带来了暴力和死亡,而这些都是马贡多小镇以前从未有过的事情。奥雷良诺当上了自由党反叛分子的首领,赢得了奥雷良诺·布恩地亚上校的称号。但是布恩地亚上校领导的反抗斗争给马贡多小镇带来的灾难是不可挽回的,自此,马贡多从一个田园式、梦幻般与世隔绝的世外桃源变成了一个与外界有着千丝万缕联系的小镇。在内战爆发期间以及内战结束之后,马贡多小镇的政权经历了屡次更迭。在其中某一时期,布恩地亚家族中出现了一位残酷的暴君——阿卡迪奥。由于阿卡迪奥推行暴政,最后被行刑队枪决。后来政府重新

ONE HUNDRED YEARS OF SOLITUDE

and his reign is peaceful until another civil uprising has him killed. After his death, the civil war ends with the signing of a peace treaty.

More than a century goes by over the course of the book, and so most of the events that García Márquez describes are the major turning points in the lives of the Buendías: births, deaths, marriages, love affairs. Some of the Buendía men are wild and sexually rapacious, frequenting brothels and taking lovers. Others are quiet and solitary, preferring to shut themselves up in their rooms to make tiny golden fish or to pore over ancient manuscripts. The women, too, range from the outrageously outgoing, like Meme, who once brings home seventy-two friends from boarding school, to the prim and proper Fernanda del Carpio, who wears a special nightgown with a hole at the crotch when she consummates her marriage with her husband.

A sense of the family's destiny for greatness remains alive in its tenacious matriarch, Ursula Iguarán, and she works devotedly to keep the family together despite its differences. But for the Buendía family, as for the entire village of Macondo, the centrifugal forces of modernity are devastating. Imperialist capitalism reaches Macondo as a banana plantation moves in and exploits the land and the workers, and the Americans who own the plantation settle in their own fenced-in section of town. Eventually, angry at the inhumane way in which they are treated, the banana workers go on strike. Thousands of them are massacred by the army, which sides with the planta-tion owners. When the bodies have been dumped into the sea, five

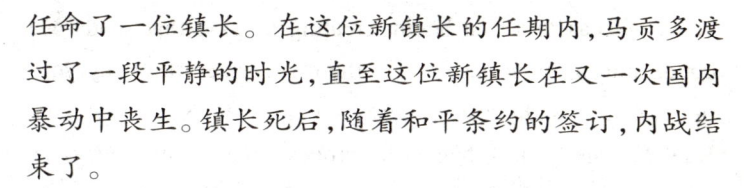

任命了一位镇长。在这位新镇长的任期内,马贡多渡过了一段平静的时光,直至这位新镇长在又一次国内暴动中丧生。镇长死后,随着和平条约的签订,内战结束了。

《百年孤独》叙述了长达一百多年的历史,作者加西亚·马尔克斯在小说中描写的大多数重大事件都是布恩地亚家族命运的转折点:降生、死亡、结婚以及乱伦。布恩地亚家族中的一些男人桀骜不驯、性欲旺盛,他们经常光顾妓院,到处拈花惹草;其他男人则性格内敛、孤独,喜欢把自己关进屋子制作小金鱼或者把全部精力倾注在古老手稿的破译上。同样在女性当中,也有性格怪异的各色人等。比如肆无忌惮、蛮横无理的梅梅,她曾经把72个寄宿学校的朋友带回家中狂欢;还有古板、一本正经的菲兰达·德卡皮奥,她在与丈夫的婚姻生活中总是穿着一个特制的睡袍,这个睡袍在两腿分叉的地方开有一个又大又圆的窟窿。

一种家族的荣耀感始终驻留在乌苏拉·伊瓜兰的意识当中。乌苏拉不仅是一位顽强的女族长而且还是家族的守护神。她竭尽全力把犹如一盘散沙的家族组织起来。但是对于布恩地亚家族和马贡多小镇来说,现代化的离心力给他们的打击是毁灭性的。殖民主义者侵入马贡多小镇,强占土地、剥削工人,把马贡多变成了香蕉种植园。拥有种植园的美国殖民者居住在他们自己的地盘内,并用篱笆把他们的居住区围建起来。终于,香蕉工人无法忍受惨无人道的剥削,他们愤怒地走上街头进行罢工。与种植园主串通一气的政府派遣部队屠杀了几千名罢工者。当罢工者的尸体被抛

ONE HUNDRED YEARS OF SOLITUDE

years of ceaseless rain begin, creating a flood that sends Macondo into its final decline. As the city, beaten down by years of violence and false progress, begins to slip away, the Buendía family, too, begins its process of final erasure, overcome by nostalgia for bygone days. The book ends almost as it began: the village is once again solitary, isolated. The few remaining Buendía family members turn in upon themselves incestuously, alienated from the outside world and doomed to a solitary ending. In the last scene of the book, the last surviving Buendía translates a set of ancient prophecies and finds that all has been predicted: that the village and its inhabitants have merely been living out a preordained cycle, incorporating great beauty and great, tragic sadness.

进大海里的时候,天上下起了绵延不断的大雨。大雨一直下了五年,洪水把马贡多冲向了彻底的衰败。至此,经受了多年战乱的蹂躏和盲目的发展之后,马贡多小镇开始走向消亡。而与此同时,布恩地亚家族也陷入了家道中落的进程,依靠缅怀过去的美好时光来舔舐心灵的创伤。小说的结尾呼应了开头:马贡多小镇经历轮回之后,回归了早期孤独、与世隔绝的状态。布恩地亚家族最后幸存下来的成员最终以乱伦、与世隔绝以及孤独的下场告终。在小说的结尾,最后一个幸存下来的布恩地亚家族成员最终破译了古老的手稿并且发现所有发生的一切早已在手稿中被预言了:马贡多小镇以及它的居民,生活在命中注定的轮回中,他们命运的轮回里交织着凄美和哀伤。

CHARACTER LIST

A Note About the Names

One of the themes of *One Hundred Years of Solitude* is the way history repeats itself in cycles. In this novel, each generation is condemned to repeat the mistakes—and to celebrate the triumphs—of the previous generation. To dramatize this point, García Márquez has given his protagonists, the Buendía family members, a very limited selection of names. *One Hundred Years of Solitude* spans six generations, and in each generation, the men of the Buendía line are Named José Arcadio or Aureliano and the women are named Úrsula, Amaranta, or Remedios. Telling the difference between people who have the same name can sometimes be difficult. To a certain extent, this is to be expected: after all, García Márquez's point is precisely that human nature does not really change, that the Buendía family is locked into a cycle of repetitions. To preserve a clear notion of the plot progression, however, it is important to pay attention to the full names of the protagonists, which often contain slight distinguishing variations. José Arcadio Buendía, for instance, is a very different character than his son, José Arcadio: although it is true that José Arcadio's last name is also "Buendía," he is never referred to, either by García Márquez or in this SparkNote, as anything but "José Arcadio." And so on.

In cases where two characters are referred to by the exact same name (for instance, Aureliano Segundo's son is also known as "José Arcadio"), we have added a roman numeral to

角色·亮相

关于名字的注释

《百年孤独》所表达的主题之一就是历史在轮回中循环往复。在小说中,每一代人都注定要重复上一代人的错误——当然也有快乐。为了突出这一点,加西亚·马尔克斯给小说的主人公们——布恩地亚家族的成员——名字的选择非常有限。《百年孤独》小说的叙述时间跨越了六代人。在每一代人当中,布恩地亚家族的男性都被命名为霍塞·阿卡迪奥或者奥雷良诺;而女性则全部被命名为乌苏拉、阿玛兰塔或者蕾麦黛丝。因此,这会给读者区分两个同名的人物造成困难。从某种程度上说,这正是预期的效果,毕竟加西亚·马尔克斯想表达这个观点:人性是难以改变的,布恩地亚家族处于循环往复的轮回之中。然而为了保持一个清晰的情节线索,记清主人公的全名是非常重要的,因为这些名字其中往往隐含着细微的差别。例如与儿子霍塞·阿卡迪奥相比,父亲霍塞·阿卡迪奥·布恩地亚是一个完全不同的角色。毋庸置疑,尽管霍塞·阿卡迪奥也姓"布恩地亚",但是作者加西亚·马尔克斯和本书都未提及他的姓氏,只是称呼他"霍塞·阿卡迪奥"。其他角色的名字也具备这种特点。

如果提及两个名字完全一样的角色(例如奥雷良诺·塞康多的儿子也叫"霍塞·阿卡迪奥"),我们在角色的名字后面加上一个罗马数字以示区别。尽管加

the character's name for the sake of clarity, even though that roman numeral does not appear in García Márquez's book: the second José Arcadio, then, appears as José Arcadio (II). Keep in mind that José Arcadio (II) is not the son of the first José Arcadio; he is merely the second José Arcadio in the book.

The Buendía Family

First Generation

José Arcadio Buendía

The patriarch of the Buendía clan, José Arcadio Buendía is Macondo's founder and its most charismatic citizen. He is a man of great strength and curiosity. Impulsively, he embarks on mad pursuits of esoteric and practical knowledge, and it is his solitary and obsessive quest for knowledge that drives him mad at the end of his life; he spends many years, in the end, tied to a tree in the Buendía backyard, speaking Latin that only the priest understands. José Arcadio Buendía is married to Úrsula Iguarán and the father of José Arcadio, Colonel Aureliano Buendía, and Amaranta.

Úrsula Iguarán

The tenacious matriarch of the Buendía clan, Úrsula lives to be well over a hundred years old, continuing with her hardheaded common sense to try and preserve the family. Every now and then, when things get particularly run-down, Úrsula

西亚·马尔克斯的原著里并没有出现过罗马数字,但是为了分清角色,采取这样的做法是有必要的。例如,第二个叫做霍塞·阿卡迪奥的角色就可以这样来表示:霍塞·阿卡迪奥(II)。值得注意的是,霍塞·阿卡迪奥(II)不是第一个霍塞·阿卡迪奥的儿子;在小说中,他仅仅是指第二个叫做霍塞·阿卡迪名字的人。

布恩地亚家族

第一代

霍塞·阿卡迪奥·布恩地亚

布恩地亚家族的族长、马贡多小镇的创建者,也是小镇居民中具有超凡魅力的人物。他气度非凡,好奇心强。不论是深奥,还是实用的知识,他都会冲动地陷入疯狂的探索之中。正是由于他孤独的性格以及对知识永无止境的追求,最终导致他晚年发疯了。发了疯以后,他被捆绑在家里后院的一棵树上,他的余生就是在这颗捆绑他的树上度过的,说着一些只有牧师才能听懂的拉丁语。霍塞·阿卡迪奥·布恩地亚娶乌苏拉·伊瓜兰为妻,是霍塞·阿卡迪奥、奥雷良诺·布恩地亚上校以及阿玛兰塔的父亲。

乌苏拉·伊瓜兰

布恩地亚家族中顽强的女族长,活了100多岁。她以顽强的意志竭尽全力地维护着这个家族。每当家族面临危机时,她总能在关键时刻身体力行、出谋划

revitalizes the family both physically and emotionally, repairing the Buendía house and breathing new life into the family. She is the wife of José Arcadio Buendía and the mother of José Arcadio, Colonel Aureliano Buendía, and Amaranta.

Second Generation

Amaranta

The daughter of Úrsula Iguarán and José Arcadio Buendía, Amaranta dies an embittered and lonely virgin. She bears deep jealousy and hatred for Rebeca, whom, she believes, stole Pietro Crespi from her. In many ways her life is characterized by a fear of men; when Pietro Crespi finally falls in love with her, she rejects him, and he kills himself. As penance, she gives herself a bad burn on the hand and wears a black bandage over it for the rest of her life. When she is much older, she finds real love with Colonel Gerineldo Márquez, but she spurns him because of her ancient fear and bitterness. She is also the object of the unconsummated incestuous passion of Aureliano José, whom she helped to raise. Amaranta is the sister of Colonel Aureliano Buendía and José Arcadio.

Colonel Aureliano Buendía

The second son of José Arcadio Buendía and Úrsula Iguarán. Aureliano grows up solitary and enigmatic, with a strange capacity for extrasensory perception. Outraged by the corruption of the Conservative government, he joins the Liber-

策,使家族重获新生。她时常修缮宅第,接纳新的家庭成员。她嫁给了霍塞·阿卡迪奥·布恩地亚,是霍塞·阿卡迪奥、奥雷良诺·布恩地亚上校以及阿玛兰塔的母亲。

第二代

阿玛兰塔

乌苏拉·伊瓜兰和霍塞·阿卡迪奥·布恩地亚的女儿。她是一个老处女,最终在痛苦和孤独中死去。她对蕾贝卡怀有深深的嫉妒和憎恨,因为她认为蕾贝卡从她身边夺走了皮埃特罗·克列斯比。她内心对男人充满了恐惧,这一点在她的生活中的诸多方面得到了体现。当皮埃特罗·克列斯比最终爱上她的时候,她拒绝了他,致使皮埃特罗·克列斯比自杀。为了忏悔,她把自己的一只手严重灼伤,然后用一条黑色的绷带缠在伤口上,至死都没有摘下来。当她日渐衰老,她找到了她的真爱——格林列尔多·马克斯上校。但是她惧怕男人和苦恼的旧病复发了,她再次拒绝了格林列尔多·马克斯。她还是奥雷良诺·霍塞乱伦欲望的对象。奥雷良诺·霍塞是由她帮助抚养长大的,他最终乱伦未遂。阿玛兰塔是奥雷良诺·布恩地亚上校和霍塞·阿卡迪奥的妹妹。

奥雷良诺·布恩地亚上校

霍塞·阿卡迪奥·布恩地亚和乌苏拉·伊瓜兰的二儿子。他从小在孤独和神秘中长大,具有异乎寻常的超感知觉能力。保守政府的腐败行为使他义愤填膺,

al rebellion and becomes Colonel Aureliano Buendía, the rebel commander. After years of fighting, he loses his capacity for memory and deep emotion, signs a peace accord, and withdraws into his workshop, a lonely and hardened man. He is the widower of Remedios Moscote and the father, with Pilar Ternera, of Aureliano José, and of seventeen sons—each named Aureliano—by seventeen different women.

Remedios Moscote

The child-bride of Colonel Aureliano Buendía, Remedios Moscote brings joy to the Buendía household for a short while before she dies suddenly, possibly of a miscarriage.

José Arcadio

The first son of Úrsula Iguarán and José Arcadio Buendía, from whom he inherits his amazing strength and his impulsive drive. After running off in pursuit of a gypsy girl, José Arcadio returns a savage brute of a man and marries Rebeca, the orphan adopted by the Buendías. He is the father, with Pilar Ternera, of Arcadio, and brother to Colonel Aureliano Buendía and Amaranta.

Rebeca

The earth-eating orphan girl who mysteriously arrives at the Buendía doorstep. Rebeca is adopted by the Buendí family. Rebeca infects the town with an insomnia that causes loss

因此义无反顾加入了自由党反叛军并且当上了反叛军的首领,号称奥雷良诺·布恩地亚上校。经历了多年的战争之后,他丧失了记忆的能力和激昂的情绪。在签署了和平协议之后,他隐居在他的试验室里,变成了一个既孤独又冷酷无情的人。他是蕾麦黛丝·摩丝柯特的鳏夫、奥雷良诺·霍塞以及17个儿子的父亲。奥雷良诺·霍塞是他与皮拉·苔列娜所生,17个儿子是他与17个不同女人所生,都起了一个相同的名字——奥雷良诺。

蕾麦黛丝·摩丝柯特

奥雷良诺·布恩地亚上校的童养媳,她的到来给布恩地亚家族的生活带来了短暂的欢乐。可能是由于小产所致,蕾麦黛丝·摩丝柯特突然去世了。

霍塞·阿卡迪奥

霍塞·阿卡迪奥·布恩地亚和乌苏拉·伊瓜兰的长子,他继承了父亲惊人的力气和冲动的性格。他不辞而别跟随一个吉普赛女孩流浪回来之后,变成了一个野兽般粗野的男人并娶了蕾贝卡为妻。蕾贝卡是布恩地亚家族收养的孤儿。霍塞·阿卡迪奥是阿卡迪奥的父亲以及奥雷良诺·布恩地亚上校和阿玛兰塔的哥哥。阿卡迪奥是他与皮拉·苔列娜所生的儿子。

蕾贝卡

一个有着吃土癖好的孤女,她带着神秘的色彩来到布恩地亚家族门前。布恩地亚家族收养了她。蕾贝

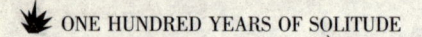

of memory. Rebeca seems to orphan herself from society and the Buendía family when, after her husband José Arcadio's death, she becomes a hermit, never seen outside her dilapidated home.

Third Generation

Aureliano José

The son of Colonel Aureliano Buendía and Pilar Ternera. Aureliano José becomes obsessed with his aunt, Amaranta, and joins his father's army when she ends the affair. He deserts the army to return to her, however, but she rejects him, horrified. He is killed by Conservative soldiers.

Arcadio

The son of José Arcadio and Pilar Ternera. Arcadio, seemingly a gentle boy, becomes schoolmaster of the town. When Colonel Aureliano Buendía places him in charge of Macondo during the uprising, however, Arcadio proves a vicious dictator who is obsessed with order. He is killed when the con—servatives retake the village. Arcadio marries Santa Sofía de la Piedad and is the father of Remedios the Beauty, Aure-liano Segundo, and José Arcadio Segundo.

Santa Sofía de la Piedad

The quiet woman, almost invisible in this novel, who

卡给全镇人传染上了失眠症,导致所有人都失去了记忆。丈夫霍塞·阿卡迪奥死后,她断绝了与外界及布恩地亚家族的联系,变成了一个孤家寡人,从此再也没有在她那摇摇欲坠的房子外面出现过。

第三代

奥雷良诺·霍塞

奥雷良诺·布恩地亚上校与皮拉·苔列娜之子,他迷恋上了他的姑姑——阿玛兰塔。当阿玛兰塔结束了他们之间的不伦之恋后,他加入了父亲的军队。但他后来弃军回到了阿玛兰塔的身边,然而被恐惧占据了的阿玛兰塔再次拒绝了他。奥雷良诺·霍塞最后被保守党士兵杀害。

阿卡迪奥

霍塞·阿卡迪奥与皮拉·苔列娜之子,他看上去好像是一个温文尔雅的男孩,后来当上了小镇的校长。然而在暴乱时期,当奥雷良诺·布恩地亚上校命令他镇守马贡多小镇的时候,他迷恋上了权力,变成了一个残酷的暴君。当保守党重新夺回小镇之后,他被枪决了。阿卡迪奥娶桑塔·索非亚·德拉佩德为妻,是俏姑娘蕾麦黛丝、奥雷良诺第二和霍塞·阿卡迪奥第二的父亲。

桑塔·索非亚·德拉佩德

小说中一个安静、几乎隐形的人物。她嫁给了阿

marries Arcadio and continues to live in the Buendía house for many years after his death, impassively tending to the family. She is the mother of Remedios the Beauty, Aureliano Segundo, and José Arcadio Segundo. She does not quite seem to exist in the real world, and when she grows old and tired, she simply walks out of the house, never to be heard from again.

Fourth Generation

Remedios the Beauty

The daughter of Santa Sofía de la Piedad and Arcadio, Remedios the Beauty becomes the most beautiful woman in the world: desire for her drives men to their deaths. Not comprehending her power over men, she remains innocent and childlike. One day, she floats to heaven, leaving Macondo and the novel abruptly.

José Arcadio Segundo

The son of Arcadio and Santa Sofía de la Piedad, José Arcadio Segundo may have been switched at birth with his twin brother, Aureliano Segundo. Appalled by witnessing an execution at an early age, José Arcadio Segundo becomes thin, bony, solitary, and increasingly scholarly, like his great-uncle Colonel Aureliano Buendía. A cockfighter and a drifter, he finds purpose in leading the strikers against the banana company. He is the lone survivor of the massacre of the strikers, and when he finds that nobody believes the massacre occurred, he secludes himself in Melquíades' old study, trying to decipher the old prophecies and preserving the memory of the

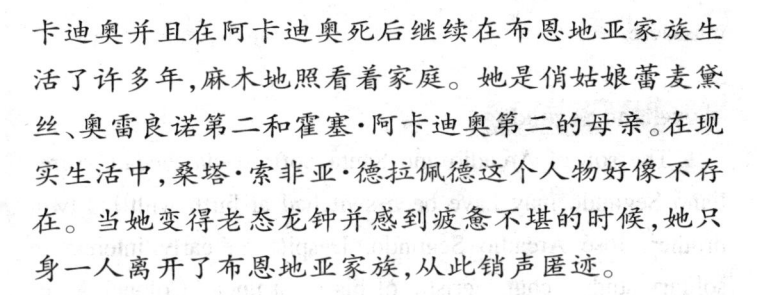

卡迪奥并且在阿卡迪奥死后继续在布恩地亚家族生活了许多年,麻木地照看着家庭。她是俏姑娘蕾麦黛丝、奥雷良诺第二和霍塞·阿卡迪奥第二的母亲。在现实生活中,桑塔·索非亚·德拉佩德这个人物好像不存在。当她变得老态龙钟并感到疲惫不堪的时候,她只身一人离开了布恩地亚家族,从此销声匿迹。

第四代

俏姑娘蕾麦黛丝

桑塔·索非亚·德拉佩德和阿卡迪奥的长女,她是世界上最美的姑娘。许多男人为了获得她而付出了生命。她意识不到她对男人具有致命的吸引力,始终保持着纯真和孩子般的天真烂漫。一天,她突然升上天空,离开了马贡多小镇并从小说中消失了。

霍塞·阿卡迪奥·塞贡多

阿卡迪奥和桑塔·索非亚·德拉佩德的次子,他和双胞胎弟奥雷良诺第二在出生时可能被调换了。霍塞·阿卡迪奥在小时候看见行刑而受了惊吓,他面容清瘦、瘦骨嶙峋、性格孤僻,学究气越来越浓,很像他的祖叔父——奥雷良诺·布恩地亚上校。霍塞·阿卡迪奥爱好斗鸡,游手好闲,后来在领导工人反抗香蕉公司的罢工过程中找到了生命的意义。他是罢工大屠杀中唯一的幸存者。当他发现没有人相信发生过大屠杀时,他把自己孤立起来,沉浸在梅尔加德斯曾经从事过的研究之中,试图破译古老的预言并保存大屠杀的

ONE HUNDRED YEARS OF SOLITUDE

massacre.

Aureliano Segundo

The son of Arcadio and Santa Sofía de la Piedad, Aureliano Segundo may have been switched at birth with his twin brother, José Arcadio Segundo. Despite an early interest in solitary study—characteristic of his great-uncle, Colonel Aureliano Buendía—Aureliano Segundo begins to show all the characteristics of the family's José Arcadios: he is immense, boisterous, impulsive, and hedonistic. Although he loves the concubine Petra Cotes, he is married to the cold beauty Fernanda del Carpio, with whom he has three children: Meme, José Arcadio (II) and Amaranta Úrsula.

Fernanda del Carpio

The wife of Aureliano Segundo and the mother of Meme, José Arcadio (II), and Amaranta Úrsula. Fernanda del Carpio was raised by a family of impoverished aristocrats; she is very haughty and very religious. Her hedonistic husband does not love her and maintains his relationship with his concubine, Petra Cotes. Fernanda del Carpio, meanwhile, tries unsuccessfully to impress her sterile religion and aristocratic manners on the Buendía house.

Fifth Generation

José Arcadio (II)

The eldest child of Aureliano Segundo and Fernanda del Carpio, Úrsula decides that José Arcadio (II) is supposed to

记忆。

奥雷良诺·塞贡多

阿卡迪奥和桑塔·索非亚·德拉佩德的小儿子,他和双胞胎哥哥霍塞·阿卡迪奥·塞贡多在出生时可能被调换。奥雷良诺·塞贡多小时候喜欢独自研究事物,这一点倒是像他祖叔父——奥雷良诺·布恩地亚上校的性格,但是他后来逐渐继承了霍塞·阿卡迪奥的全部性格和特征:身材高大、性格暴躁、冲动以及追求享乐。尽管他喜欢他的情妇——佩特娜·柯特,但是他还是跟冷美人菲兰达·德卡皮奥结了婚并育有三个儿女:梅梅、霍塞·阿卡迪奥第二以及阿玛兰塔·乌苏拉。

菲兰达·德卡皮奥

奥雷良诺·塞贡多的妻子以及梅梅、霍塞·阿卡迪奥第二和阿玛兰塔·乌苏拉的母亲。菲兰达·德卡皮奥生于一个没落的贵族家庭。她高傲、宗教意识强烈。她的丈夫追求享乐,并不爱她,与情妇佩特娜·柯特始终保持着关系。菲兰达·德卡皮奥在布恩地亚家族里举行陈腐的宗教仪式,想要始终保持着她的贵族风度,但是她所做的一切都是徒劳的。

第五代

霍塞·阿卡迪奥第二

奥雷良诺·塞贡多和菲兰达·德卡皮奥的长子。乌苏拉认定霍塞·阿卡迪奥第二将来会当上教皇,但是

become the Pope, but he in fact slides into dissolution and solitude. On his return from his unsuccessful trip to seminary in Italy, José Arcadio (II) leads a life of debauchery with local adolescents who eventually murder him and steal his money.

Amaranta Úrsula

The daughter of Aureliano Segundo and Fernanda del Carpio, Amaranta Úrsula returns from her trip to Europe with a Belgian husband, Gaston. She wants to revitalize Macondo and the Buendía household, but it is too late: both are headed for inevitable ruin. She falls in love with her nephew, Aureliano (II), and gives birth to his child, whom they also name Aureliano (III) and who proves the last in the Buendía line. Born of incest, he has the tail of a pig. Amaranta dies in childbirth.

Gaston

The Belgian husband of Amaranta Úrsula, Gaston is loving and cultured but feels isolated in the now-desolate Macondo. He travels to Belgium to start an airmail company, and, when he hears of the relationship between his wife and Aureliano (II), he never returns.

Meme

The daughter of Fernanda del Carpio and Aureliano Segundo, Meme's real name is Renata Remedios. She feigns studiousness and docility to please her mother, but she is actu-

实际上霍塞·阿卡迪奥第二是一个自甘堕落、性格孤僻的人。他前往意大利神学院求学,但是最后无果而终,返回了马贡多,和当地一撮小青年过着奢侈淫逸的生活。这伙小青年为了劫取他的钱财,最终将他谋杀了。

阿玛兰塔·乌苏拉

奥雷良诺·塞贡多和菲兰达·德卡皮奥的女儿。欧洲旅行结束后,她偕同比利时丈夫加斯东一起返回家中。她企图复兴马贡多小镇和布恩地亚家族,但为时已晚:马贡多小镇和布恩地亚家族已经走向了不可避免的毁灭。她与侄子——奥雷良诺第二坠入爱河,并且生下了他的孩子。他们给孩子同样取名为奥雷良诺(第三)——布恩地亚家族的最后一代人。由于是乱伦所生,奥雷良诺第三身上长了一只猪尾巴,阿玛兰塔·乌苏拉也在分娩中死去。

加斯东

阿玛兰塔·乌苏拉的比利时丈夫。他重感情、有涵养,但是他在满目疮痍的马贡多感到非常孤独。他打算到比利时开办航空邮政公司。当知道了妻子与奥雷良诺第二的乱伦关系之后,他就再也没有回来。

梅梅

菲兰达·德卡皮奥和奥雷良诺·塞贡多的女儿,真名叫蕾纳塔·蕾麦黛丝。为了博得母亲的欢心,她佯装好学、顺从安排,但是实际上她和父亲一样,喜欢追求

ally a hedonist like her father. When her mother discovers her illicit affair with Mauricio Babilonia, she posts a guard in front of the house; the guard ends up shooting Mauricio. He ends up paralyzed, and Meme is imprisoned in a convent where she spends the rest of her life. The product of her affair with Babilonia is Aureliano (II).

Sixth Generation

Aureliano (II)

The illegitimate son of Meme and Mauricio Babilonia, Aureliano (II) is concealed by his scandalized grandmother, Fernanda del Carpio. He grows up a hermit in the Buendía household, only gradually acclimating himself to society. Aureliano (II) becomes a scholar, and it is he who eventually deciphers the prophecies of Melquíades. With his aunt, Amaranta Úrsula, he fathers the last in the Buendía line, the baby Aureliano (III), who dies soon after birth.

Characters who are not members of the Buendía Family

Melquíades

The gypsy who brings technological marvels to Macondo and befriends the Buendía clan. Melquíades is the first person to die in Macondo. Melquíades serves as José Arcadio Buendía's guide in his quest for knowledge and, even after dying, returns to guide other generations of Buendías. Melquíades' mysterious and undecipherable prophecies, which torment generations of Buendías, are finally translated by Au-

享乐。当她的母亲发现她与毛里西奥·巴比洛尼亚私通之后，便在房前派设了一名警卫。警卫最后用枪打伤了毛里西奥，致使毛里西奥·巴比洛尼亚终生瘫痪，而梅梅则遭到监禁并在女修道院度过了余生。奥雷良诺第二的降生是她和巴比洛尼亚偷情的结果。

第六代

奥雷良诺第二

梅梅和毛里西奥·巴比洛尼亚的私生子。他的祖母菲兰达·德卡皮奥因他而感到耻辱，因此把他隐藏在布恩地亚家族里。他从小在隐密中长大，后来才逐渐公开了身份。奥雷良诺第二成为一个学者，是他最终破译了梅尔加德斯的预言。他和姨妈阿玛兰塔·乌苏拉生下了布恩地亚家族中最后一代人——奥雷良诺第三。奥雷良诺第三出生后不久便死了。

非布恩地亚家族成员角色

梅尔加德斯

梅尔加德斯是吉普赛人。他带着各种稀奇古怪的技术来到马贡多并且和布恩地亚家族交上了朋友。梅尔加德斯是第一个在马贡多小镇死亡的人。他指引霍塞·阿卡迪奥·布恩地亚在知识的海洋中探索，即使死后，仍以显灵的方式来指导布恩地亚家族的其他后代。在小说结尾，梅尔加德斯神秘而无法破解的预言

reliano (II) at the end of the novel—they contain the entire history of Macondo, foretold.

Pilar Ternera

A local whore and madam. With José Arcadio, Pilar is the mother of Arcadio; with Colonel Aureliano Buendía, she is the mother of Aureliano José. She is also a fortune-teller whose quiet wisdom helps guide the Buendía family. She survives until the very last days of Macondo.

Petra Cotes

Aureliano Segundo's concubine. Petra Cotes and Aureliano Segundo become extremely rich—their own love seems to inspire their animals to procreate unnaturally quickly. Even after the poverty caused by the flood, she stays with Aureliano Segundo; their deepened love is one of the purest emotions in the novel.

Mauricio Babilonia

The sallow, solemn lover of Meme. Fernanda del Carpio disapproves of their affair, and she sets up a guard who shoots Mauricio Babilonia when he attempts to climb into the house for a tryst with Meme. As a result, Mauricio lives the rest of his life completely paralyzed. He fathers Meme's child, Aureliano (II).

终于被奥雷良诺第二破解了。这些曾经折磨一代又一代布恩地亚家族后人的预言预示了马贡多小镇的整部历史。

皮拉·苔列娜

一个当地的娼妓和老鸨。她和霍塞·阿卡迪奥生下了阿卡迪奥,和奥雷良诺·布恩地亚上校生下了奥雷良诺·霍塞。她还是一个会算命的人,她异乎寻常的智慧曾经指引过布恩地亚家族。她一直活到了马贡多小镇的末日。

佩特纳·柯特

奥雷良诺·塞贡多的情妇。她和奥雷良诺·塞贡多获得了惊人的财富——他们之间的情欲似乎刺激了他们饲养的牲畜以异乎寻常的速度快速繁殖。即使在洪水引发的贫困之时,佩特纳·柯特与奥雷良诺·塞贡多始终同甘共苦。他们之间的真挚感情是小说中最纯洁的情感之一。

毛里西奥·巴比洛尼亚

梅梅的情人,他面色发黄、神色忧郁。菲兰达·德卡皮奥不赞同他们之间的私情并且派设了一名看护的警卫。当毛里西奥·巴比洛尼亚试图翻进屋里与梅梅幽会时,警卫用枪打伤了他。结果,毛里西奥在瘫痪中度过了余生。他和梅梅生了一个儿子——奥雷良诺第二。

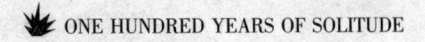

Pietro Crespi

The gentle, delicate Italian musician who is loved by both Amaranta and Rebeca. Rebeca, however, chooses to marry the more manly José Arcadio. After Amaranta leads on Pietro and rejects him, Pietro commits suicide.

Colonel Gerineldo Márquez

The comrade-in-arms of Colonel Aureliano Buendía. Colonel Gerineldo is the first to become tired of the civil war. He falls in love with Amaranta, who spurns him.

Don Apolinar Moscote

Father of Remedios Moscote and government-appointed magistrate of Macondo. Don Apolinar Moscote is a Conservative and helps rig the election so that his party will win. His dishonesty is partly why Colonel Aureliano Buendía first joins the Liberals.

皮埃特罗·克列斯比

来自于意大利的一个温文尔雅、性格脆弱的音乐家。阿玛兰塔和蕾贝卡都爱上了他。然而蕾贝卡却选择嫁给了更具男子气概的霍塞·阿卡迪奥。皮埃特罗·克列斯比后来受到了阿玛兰塔的诱惑，但随之又被她拒绝，皮埃特罗因此自杀。

格林列尔多·马克斯上校

奥雷良诺·布恩地亚上校的战友，他是第一个厌倦了内战的人。他爱上了阿玛兰塔，但是阿玛兰塔最后轻蔑地拒绝了他。

唐·阿波利纳尔·摩丝柯特

蕾麦黛丝·摩丝柯特的父亲。他被政府指派到马贡多担任行政长官。唐·阿波利纳尔·摩丝柯特是一个保守派分子，他暗箱操作以便帮助保守派获取选举的胜利。他的伪善是奥雷良诺·布恩地亚上校第一个加入自由党的部分原因。

ANALYSIS OF MAJOR CHARACTERS

José Arcadio Buendía

The founder and patriarch of Macondo, José Arcadio Buendía represents both great leadership and the innocence of the ancient world. He is a natural explorer, setting off into the wilderness first to found Macondo and then to find a route between Macondo and the outside world. In this tale of creation he is the Adam figure, whose quest for knowledge, mirrored in the intellectual pursuits of his descendants, eventually results in his family's loss of innocence. José Arcadio Buendía pushes his family forward into modernity, preferring the confines of his laboratory to the sight of a real flying carpet that the gypsies have brought. By turning his back on this ancient magic in favor of his more modern scientific ideas, he hastens the end of Macondo's Eden-like state.

For José Arcadio Buendía, however, madness comes sooner than disillusionment. Immediately after he thinks he has discovered a means to create perpetual motion—a physical impossibility—he goes insane, convinced that the same day is repeating itself over and over again. In a sense, his purported discovery of perpetual motion achieves a kind of total knowledge that may be too deep for the human mind to withstand. Perpetual motion could only exist in a world without time, which, for José Arcadio Buendía, is what the world becomes and, in a sense, is what time throughout the novel becomes: past, pre-

主角·赏

霍塞·阿卡迪奥·布恩地亚

霍塞·阿卡迪奥·布恩地亚是马贡多小镇的创建者和族长,在一个蒙昧的时代,他既是权威的象征,又是纯真的化身。他是一个天生的探险家,在一片荒野之中创建了马贡多小镇,紧接着又开始探索一条从马贡多通往外界的通道。在这部小说里,他被赋予了亚当的形象。他的后代对知识的追求折射了他的这种探索精神,而正是因为他们对知识永无止境的探索导致他的家族逐渐失去了纯真。霍塞·阿卡迪奥·布恩地亚推动着他的家族向现代化发展,他把自己囚禁在实验室里,企图把吉普赛人带来的毛毯变成真正会飞的飞毯。后来他放弃了这个古老的神话,倾向于研究更加现代化的科学技术——由此他加速了马贡多伊甸园般状态的终结。

然而对于霍塞·阿卡迪奥·布恩地亚来说,发疯比幻想的破灭来的还要早。在他自认为发现了一种能够产生永恒运动的方法——这在物理学上是不可能的——之后不久,他便发疯了。他确信同一天总是在不断地重复着。在某种意义上说,他发明的永恒运动原理达到了一种全知的境界,这种全知可能太深奥了,以致人无法理解它。永恒运动只有在没有时间的状态下才能存在,而这对于霍塞·阿卡迪奥·布恩地亚来说就是世界存在的状态,在某种程度上说也就是时

sent and future often overlap. This overlapping of time allows José Arcadio Buendía to appear to his descendants in the form of a ghost, so that his presence will always be felt in Macondo.

Colonel Aureliano Buendía

Colonel Aureliano Buendía is *One Hundred Years of Solitude's* greatest soldier figure, leading the Liberal army throughout the civil war. At the same time, however, he is the novel's greatest artist figure: a poet, an accomplished silversmith, and the creator of hundreds of finely crafted golden fishes. Aureliano's (I) inability to experience deep emotion contributes to his great battle poise and artistic focus, yet Márquez's depiction of the Colonel melting away his hard work and starting all over again signals that this poise and focus is not worth its price.

Aureliano (I) is never truly touched by anything or anyone. His child bride, Remedios Moscote, seems at first to have a real effect on him. When she dies, however, he discovers that his sorrow is not as profound as he had expected. During the war, he becomes even more hardened to emotion, and, eventually, his memory and all his feelings are worn away. He has all of his poems burned, and, by the end of his life, he has stopped making new golden fish. Instead, he makes twenty-five and then melts them down, using the metal for the next batch. In this way, he lives solely in the present, acknowledging that time moves in cycles and that the present is all that exists for a man like him, with no memories.

间在整部小说中所存在的状态：过去、现在和未来常常重叠在一起。这种时间上的重叠让霍塞·阿卡迪奥·布恩地亚的幽灵经常出现在他的后代面前，以至于整个马贡多小镇总能感觉到他的存在。

奥雷良诺·布恩地亚上校

奥雷良诺·布恩地亚上校是《百年孤独》小说中最伟大的斗士形象，他领导自由党部队在内战中南征北战。同时，他又是小说中最伟大的艺术家形象，他是一个诗人，又是一个有造诣的银器匠，精心制作了数以百计的小金鱼。正是他冷酷无情的性格造就了他伟大的斗士形象和高深的艺术造诣。然而马尔克斯描写布恩地亚上校溶化掉自己的全部作品然后重新再来，说明拥有这种形象和造诣对于布恩地亚上校来说是毫无意义的。

从来没有任何事情或者任何人真正地打动过奥雷良诺第一（奥雷良诺·布恩地亚上校）。他的童养媳——蕾麦黛丝·摩丝柯特起初似乎对他有过真正的触动，然而当蕾麦黛丝·摩丝柯特死去时，他发现他的悲伤并没有他事先预料得那样沉痛。在战争时期，他变得更加铁石心肠，最终丧失了记忆，感情也耗费殆尽。他焚毁了自己所有的诗稿。在暮年，他停止制作新的小金鱼。相反，他只制作25只小金鱼，然后把它们溶化掉，再用溶化掉的金子制作下一批小金鱼。他就这样孤独地活在现在，承认时间在循环中往复，对于像他这样没有记忆的人来说，一切都只存在于现在。

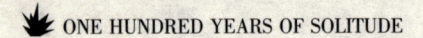

Colonel Aureliano Buendía's attempted suicide shows us how deep his despair is when he realizes that civil war is futile and that pride is the only thing that keeps the two sides fighting. His disillusionment is a moving commentary on the despair that arises from futility but, also, on the futility that arises from despair.

Úrsula Iguarán

Of all the characters in the novel, Úrsula Iguarán lives the longest and sees the most new generations born. She outlives all three of her children. Unlike most of her relatives, Úrsula is untroubled by great spiritual anxiety; in this sense, she is probably the strongest person ever to live in Macondo. She takes in Rebeca, the child of strangers, and raises her as her own daughter; she welcomes dozens of passing strangers to her table; she tries to keep the house from falling apart. Úrsula's task is not easy, since all of her descendants become embroiled in wars and scandals that would cause any weaker family to dissolve. With Ursula as their mainstay, however, the Buendías are irrevocably linked, for better or for worse. To keep the family together, Úrsula sometimes is quite harsh; for example, she kicks José Arcadio and Rebeca out of the house when they elope. This decision is partly a result of her unyielding fear of incest. Even though Rebeca and José Arcadio are not technically related, Úrsula is terrified that even a remotely incestuous action or relation will result in someone in the family having a baby with the tail of a pig. Her own marriage to José Arcadio Buendía is incestuous because they are cousins, and she constantly examines her children's behavior for flaws, frequently saying, "[i]t's worse than if he had been born with the tail of

当奥雷良诺·布恩地亚上校意识到内战是徒劳的，导致双方战斗的惟一原因仅仅是出于傲慢时，他失望透顶，想要自杀。这一点说明他理想的破灭是源于他对徒劳产生的失望，同时又是源于由失望而产生的徒劳。

乌苏拉·伊瓜兰

在小说所有的角色中，乌苏拉·伊瓜兰是寿命最长的一个，她几乎亲眼目睹了每一代人的出生。她的寿命超过了她的三个子女。不像大多数其他家族成员，乌苏拉从未被巨大的精神困扰所难倒，从这个角度讲她也许是马贡多小镇有史以来最顽强的人。她收养了陌生人的孩子蕾贝卡，并把她当作自己的女儿抚养成人；她曾经邀请数十个陌生的过客到家中吃饭；她竭尽全力防止家族的分裂。这可不是一件容易的活儿，儿孙们要么卷入战争，要么牵连丑闻，而这些都会导致家族的分崩离析。作为家族的中流砥柱，不论好坏，她总是能把家族成员紧密地联系在一起。为了保护整个家族，乌苏拉有时会采用非常严厉的手段。比如，当霍塞·阿卡迪奥和蕾贝卡私通时，她把他们赶出了家门。她这么做的部分原因是由于她对乱伦具有无法抑制的恐惧感。尽管蕾贝卡和霍塞·阿卡迪奥并没有血缘关系，但是乌苏拉还是担心即使是远亲，乱伦照样会导致家里人生出一个长着猪尾的孩子。由于她和丈夫霍塞·阿卡迪奥·布恩地亚是表兄妹，因此他和丈夫的婚姻也是乱伦关系。她经常从孩子们的一举一动当中寻找各种生理缺陷并且常常说："这比出生时

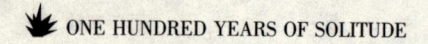

a pig." Because of her fear of incest, Úrsula is a contradictory character: she binds the family together, but is terrified that incest, the extreme of family bonding, will bring disaster to the Buendía house.

Aureliano (II)

Aureliano (II) is the purest example in *One Hundred Years of Solitude* of the solitary, destructive Buendía thirst for knowledge. He is utterly isolated by his grandmother, Fernanda del Carpio, because she is ashamed that he was born out of wedlock. He never even leaves the house until he is fully grown. As he lives in solitude, however, he acquires a store of knowledge almost magical in scope. He knows far more than he could have read in his family's books and seems to have miraculously accessed an enormous store of universal knowledge. After having an incestuous relationship with his aunt, Amaranta Úrsula, Aureliano (II) watches the last of the Buendía line (their son, born with the tail of a pig) being eaten by ants. He finally translates the prophecies of the old gypsy, Melquíades, which foretell both the act of translation and the destruction of Macondo that occurs as he reads. Aureliano (II) is therefore Macondo's prophet of doom, destroying the town with an act of reading and translation that is similar to our reading of *One Hundred Years of Solitude*.

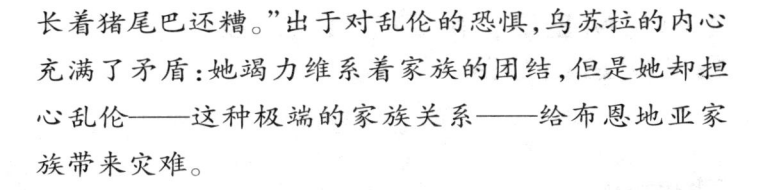

长着猪尾巴还糟。"出于对乱伦的恐惧,乌苏拉的内心充满了矛盾:她竭力维系着家族的团结,但是她却担心乱伦——这种极端的家族关系——给布恩地亚家族带来灾难。

奥雷良诺第二

在《百年孤独》小说中,奥雷良诺第二是最典型的孤独的代表:他性格孤僻,渴望知识,最终毁灭了布恩地亚家族。由于他是一个私生子,他的祖母——菲兰达·德卡皮奥因他而感到耻辱,因此他完全被祖母藏匿起来。直到他长大成人,他甚至从来没有走出过家门一步。然而正是因为在孤独中长大,他获取了大量的知识,掌控知识的领域几乎达到了无所不包的程度。他掌握的知识远远超过了他在家中书籍里所学过的东西,并且似乎能够奇迹般地汲取宇宙间浩瀚如烟的知识。他与自己姨妈阿玛兰塔·乌苏拉发生乱伦关系并且目睹了布恩地亚家族的最后一代(他们的儿子——出生时长着猪尾)被蚂蚁吞噬了。他最终破译了老吉普赛人梅尔加德斯的预言。当他阅读预言时,他发现预言既预示了他破译预言的行为又预示了马贡多的毁灭。如同我们阅读《百年孤独》一样,奥雷良诺第二是马贡多小镇命运的预言者,正是他阅读和破译预言的行为毁灭了马贡多小镇。

THEMES, MOTIFS & SYMBOLS

Themes

Themes are the fundamental and often universal ideas explored in a literary work.

The Subjectivity of Experienced Reality

Although the realism and the magic that *One Hundred Years of Solitude* includes seem at first to be opposites, they are, in fact, perfectly reconcilable. Both are necessary in order to convey Márquez's particular conception of the world. Márquez's novel reflects reality not as it is experienced by one observer, but as it is individually experienced by those with different backgrounds. These multiple perspectives are especially appropriate to the unique reality of Latin America—caught between modernity and pre-industrialization; torn by civil war, and ravaged by imperialism—where the experiences of people vary much more than they might in a more homogenous society. Magical realism conveys a reality that incorporates the magic that superstition and religion infuse into the world.

This novel treats biblical narratives and native Latin American mythology as historically credible. This approach may stem from the sense, shared by some Latin American authors, that important and powerful strains of magic running

主题·主题成分·象征

主题

主题是一部文学作品所探索的基本的、常常是带有普遍性的思想。

现实经历的主观性

《百年孤独》同时含有现实主义和魔幻主义的成分,尽管这两种成分起初看似相互矛盾,但是事实上它们能够完美地调和在一起。为了表达马尔克斯独特的世界观,这两种成分的应用是必要的。马尔克斯的小说不仅反映了某一个旁观者所经历的的现实,而是也反映了那些有着不同背景的人各自所经历的现实。对于当时正处在现代化与前工业化转型时期的拉丁美洲来说,采用这种多视角叙事方式来反映拉美独特的社会现实是再也合适不过的。在这个遭受了内战百般蹂躏以及殖民主义疯狂掠夺的国家里,民众所遭受的经历与他们在一个具有单一特征的社会里可能的经历比起来是非常不同的。魔幻现实主义表达一种现实,这种现实融合了魔幻的成分,而魔幻的世界里又充满了迷信和宗教的色彩。

小说把圣经故事和拉美本土神话视作可信的史实。这种创作手法来源于一种观点:即魔幻在拉美人民日常生活当中所起到的重要和强有力的作用已被西方世界所强调的逻辑和理性所消解,这个观点已得

through ordinary lives fall victim to the Western emphasis on logic and reason. If García Márquez seems to confuse reality and fiction, it is only because, from some perspectives, fiction may be truer than reality, and vice versa. For instance, in places like Márquez's hometown, which witnessed a massacre much like that of the workers in Macondo, unthinkable horrors may be a common sight. Real life, then, begins to seem like a fantasy that is both terrifying and fascinating, and Márquez's novel is an attempt to recreate and to capture that sense of real life.

The Inseparability of Past, Present, and Future

From the names that return generation after generation to the repetition of personalities and events, time in One Hundred Years of Solitude refuses to divide neatly into past, present, and future. Úrsula Iguarán is always the first to notice that time in Macondo is not finite, but, rather, moves forward over and over again. Sometimes, this simultaneity of time leads to amnesia, when people cannot see the past any more than they can see the future. Other times the future becomes as easy to recall as the past. The prophecies of Melquíades prove that events in time are continuous: from the beginning of the novel, the old gypsy was able to see its end, as if the various events were all occurring at once. Similarly, the presence of the ghosts of Melquíades and José Arcadio Buendía shows that the past in which those men lived has become one with the present.

The Power of Reading and of Language

Although language is in an unripe, Garden-of-Eden state

到了一些拉美作家的认可。如果加西亚·马尔克斯看似混淆现实和虚幻之间的界线，那么从某种角度上说，只是因为虚幻比现实更具真实性，反之亦然。例如，在马尔克斯的家乡，当地小镇所经历过的大屠杀与小说中马贡多工人所经历的大屠杀十分相似，令人难以置信的恐怖司空见惯。现实犹如梦幻，既使人感到恐惧又使人产生幻觉，而马尔克斯的小说试图再现和捕捉这种现实感。

过去、现在和将来的不可分离性

在《百年孤独》中，人物的名字一代一代地重复，角色的性格特征和事件也反复出现，这说明小说没有把过去、现在和未来明确地分割开来。乌苏拉·伊瓜兰第一个注意到时间在马贡多是不确定的，是循环往复式的。当人们无法区分过去和未来的时候，这种时间上的同时性会导致健忘症。在某些情况下，预见未来跟回忆过去一样的简单。梅尔加德斯的预言证明了事件在时间中是持续发展的：在小说的开头，这个老吉普赛人就已经预言了结尾，似乎不同的事件全都在同一时刻发生了。同样，梅尔加德斯和霍塞·阿卡迪奥·布恩地亚幽灵的出现说明那些生活在过去的人与现在活着的人共同存在于同一时空之中。

阅读和语言的魔力

尽管在小说的开篇，语言还是一种不成熟的、伊

at the beginning of *One Hundred Years of Solitude*, when most things in the newborn world are still unnamed, its function quickly becomes more complex. Various languages fill the novel, including the Guajiro language that the children learn, the multilingual tattoos that cover José Arcadio's body, the Latin spoken by José Arcadio Buendía, and the final Sanskrit translation of Melquíades's prophecies. In fact, this final act of translation can be seen as the most significant act in the book, since it seems to be the one that makes the book's existence possible and gives life to the characters and story within.

As García Márquez makes reading the final apocalyptic force that destroys Macondo and calls attention to his own task as a writer, he also reminds us that our reading provides the fundamental first breath to every action that takes place in *One Hundred Years of Solitude*. While the novel can be thought of as something with one clear, predetermined meaning, García Márquez asks his reader to acknowledge the fact that every act of reading is also an interpretation, and that such interpretations can have weighty consequences. Aureliano (II), then, does not just take the manuscripts' meanings for granted, but, in addition, he must also translate and interpret them and ultimately precipitate the destruction of the town.

Motifs

Motifs are recurring structures, contrasts, or literary devices that can help to develop and inform the text's major themes.

甸园式的状态,这时候大多数事物在这个新开辟的天地里还没有被命名,但是很快语言的功能开始复杂化了。小说中充满了多种语言,其中包括孩子们学习的瓜希拉语、纹于霍塞·阿卡迪奥身上的多语塔图、霍塞·阿卡迪奥·布恩地亚说的拉丁语以及梅尔加德斯预言里被破译的梵语。事实上,在小说的最后,奥雷良诺第二翻译梵语的行为可以被视作全书中最具意义的行动,因为其作用是:它使小说的存在成为可能并且给小说中的角色和故事赋予了生命。

由于加西亚·马尔克斯在小说中使阅读成为最后摧毁马贡多小镇的启示性力量,并且引起读者注意他作为作者所扮演的角色,他是在给予我们这样一个启示:我们阅读的过程即是给《百年孤独》小说中每一个发生的细节赋予最基本的原始注解的过程。我们可以把小说解读为具有明确的、预先设定好的意义。加西亚·马尔克斯让读者体会到这样一种事实:阅读小说的行为本身就是一种解读,而这种解读可以产生深远的影响。奥雷良诺第二同样没有把手稿视为理所当然,而是他必须把手稿的预言翻译、破解出来,并最终预言了小镇的毁灭。

主题成分

主题成分是指可以有助于逐步展现并形成文本主题的再现结构、对比或文学手段。

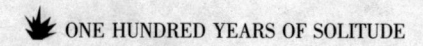

Memory and Forgetfulness

While the characters in *One Hundred Years of Solitude* consider total forgetfulness a danger, they, ironically, also seem to consider memory a burden. About half of the novel's characters speak of the weight of having too many memories while the rest seem to be amnesiacs. Rebeca's overabundance of memory causes her to lock herself in her house after her husband's death, and to live there with the memory of friends rather than the presence of people. For her, the nostalgia of better days gone by prevents her from existing in a changing world. The opposite of her character can be found in Colonel Aureliano Buendía, who has almost no memories at all. He lives in an endlessly repeating present, melting down and then recreating his collection of little gold fishes. Nostalgia and amnesia are the dual diseases of the Buendía clan, one tying its victims to the past, the other trapping them in the present. Thus afflicted, the Buendías are doomed to repeat the same cycles until they consume themselves, and they are never able to move into the future.

The Bible

One Hundred Years of Solitude draws on many of the basic narratives of the Bible, and its characters can be seen as allegorical of some major biblical figures. The novel recounts the creation of Macondo and its earliest Edenic days of innocence, and continues until its apocalyptic end, with a cleansing flood in between. We can see José Arcadio Buendía's downfall—his loss of sanity—as a result of his quest for knowledge. He and his wife, Ursula Iguarán, represent the biblical Adam and Eve, who were exiled from Eden after eating from the

记忆和忘记

《百年孤独》小说中的人物意识到健忘是一种危险,但是具有讽刺意味的是他们同时把记忆当成了一种负担。小说中约半数人物均感受到了记忆的沉重压力,然而另一些人物却处于健忘的状态。丈夫死后,蕾贝卡的沉重记忆导致她把自己与世隔绝起来,不与人接触,生活在回忆当中。由于沉湎于过去的美好日子,所以她无法适应变化中的世界。在奥雷良诺上校身上,我们发现了与蕾贝卡完全相反的性格特征:他几乎丧失了所有的记忆。奥雷良诺上校生活在永无止境的循环往复之中,他不断地把他执迷收藏的小金鱼溶化掉,然后再重新制作。布恩地亚家族染上双重疾病:怀旧和健忘。前者把病人束缚在过去,后者把病人禁锢于现在。倍受煎熬的布恩地亚家族注定要在时间的循环中往复,根本无法走向未来,直至生命耗费殆尽。

圣经

《百年孤独》小说引用了许多圣经典故,小说中的人物也被赋予了圣经中主要人物的形象。小说再现了马贡多小镇的创世纪以及小镇早期伊甸园般纯真的生活。故事情节持续发展直至马贡多小镇被预言摧毁,其间还穿插了一段大雨引发洪水的情景。我们从中看到了霍塞·阿卡迪奥·布恩地亚的堕落——他的发疯源于他对于知识的探索。他与妻子乌苏拉·伊瓜兰分别代表了圣经中的亚当和夏娃——他们由于品尝了智慧树之果,被逐出了伊甸园。整部小说隐喻了

Tree of Knowledge. The entire novel functions as a metaphor for human history and an extended commentary on human nature. On the one hand, their story, taken literally as applying to the fictional Buendías, evokes immense pathos. But as representatives of the human race, the Buendías personify solitude and inevitable tragedy, together with the elusive possibility of happiness, as chronicled by the Bible.

The Gypsies

Gypsies are present in *One Hundred Years of Solitude* primarily to act as links. They function to offer transitions from contrasting or unrelated events and characters. Every few years, especially in the early days of Macondo, a pack of wandering gypsies arrives, turning the town into something like a carnival and displaying the wares that they have brought with them. Before Macondo has a road to civilization, they are the town's only contact with the outside world. They bring both technology—inventions that Melquíades displays—and magic—magic carpets and other wonders. Gypsies, then, serve as versatile literary devices that also blur the line between fantasy and reality, especially when they connect Macondo and the outside world, magic and science, and even the past and present.

Symbols

Symbols are objects, characters, figures, or colors used to represent abstract ideas or concepts.

Little Gold Fishes

The meaning of the thousands of little gold fishes that

人类的历史并且对人性进行了进一步探讨。从一方面来说，尽管小说采用了虚构的表现方法，但是人们还是对布恩地亚家族的故事产生了极大的悲悯。作为人类的代表，如同圣经所启示的那样，布恩地亚家族代表了人类孤独的情感、不可避免的悲剧以及难以捉摸的幸福的可能性。

吉普赛人

吉普赛人为小说情节的发展起到了承上启下的作用，为不相关联的事件和人物提供了过渡。每隔几年，特别是在马贡多小镇建立的初期，一群流浪的吉普赛人就会来到马贡多，兜售他们随身带来的各种玩意儿并且把整个小镇变成了狂欢节。在马贡多与外界文明接触之前，吉普赛人是马贡多小镇与外界交往的唯一媒介。他们不仅带来了技术，例如梅尔加德斯带来的新发明，而且还带来了魔法——飞毯以及其他奇妙的东西。吉普赛人在小说中起到了文学修辞的多样性功能，特别是当他们建立了马贡多与外界的联系时，这种修辞效果模糊了幻想与现实、魔法与科学，甚至过去与未来的界限。

象征

象征是用来体现抽象思想与概念的物、人、数字符号或色彩。

小金鱼

奥雷良诺·布恩地亚上校制作了数以千计的小金

Colonel Aureliano Buendía makes shifts over time. At first, these fishes represent Aureliano's artistic nature and, by extension, the artistic nature of all the Aurelianos. Soon, however, they acquire a greater significance, marking the ways in which Aureliano has affected the world. His seventeen sons, for example, are each given a little gold fish, and, in this case, the fishes represent Aureliano's effect on the world through his sons. In another instance, they are used as passkeys when messengers for the Liberals use them to prove their allegiance. Many years later, however, the fishes become collector's items, merely relics of a once-great leader. This attitude disgusts Aureliano because he recognizes that people are using him as a figurehead, a mythological hero that represents whatever they want it to represent. When he begins to understand that the little gold fishes no longer are symbolic of him personally, but instead of a mistaken ideal, he stops making new fishes and starts to melt down the old ones again and again.

The Railroad

The railroad represents the arrival of the modern world in Macondo. This devastating turn leads to the development of a banana plantation and the ensuing massacre of three thousand workers. The railroad also represents the period when Macondo is connected most closely with the outside world. After the banana plantations close down, the railroad falls into disrepair and the train ceases even to stop in Macondo any more. The advent of the railroad is a turning point. Before it comes, Macondo grows bigger and thrives; afterward, Macondo quickly disintegrates, folding back into isolation and eventually expiring.

鱼,这些小金鱼的意义随着时间的发展而变化。起初,这些小金鱼代表着奥雷良诺上校的艺术品质,继而代表着所有叫做奥雷良诺名字的人物的艺术品质。随之不久,小金鱼被赋予了更高层面的意义——标记着奥雷良诺影响整个世界的方式。例如奥雷良诺·布恩地亚上校的17个儿子每人都获得了一条小金鱼,从这层意义上说,小金鱼代表奥雷良诺上校在世界范围内的影响,而这种影响正是通过他的儿子们产生的。另外,自由党反叛分子为了证明他们的身份,用小金鱼作为接头暗号。然而多年以后,小金鱼变成了奥雷良诺上校的收藏品:一代枭雄仅有的纪念物。当奥雷良诺上校意识到他被利用了的时候,这种被欺骗的感觉使他懊丧不已。民众只是把他当成了一个傀儡,一个神话英雄——他们理想的替身。他停止了制作新的小金鱼,开始一遍又一遍地熔化掉旧的小金鱼。

铁路

铁路代表着马贡多现代化时代的到来。马贡多进入了一个社会转型期,这个转型是毁灭性的,它带来了香蕉种植园的发展以及导致了随之而来的大屠杀,被害工人达三千之多。铁路同样代表着马贡多与外界接触最密切的一个时期。香蕉园被封之后,铁路荒废了,甚至连火车也不在马贡多停靠了。铁路时代的到来是一个转折点。没有铁路之前,马贡多的发展不仅越来越大而且越来越繁荣;而自从修铁路开通之后,马贡多就开始迅速衰败,倒回了与世隔绝的状态,以致最终逐渐消亡了。

The English Encyclopedia

At first, the English encyclopedia that Meme receives from her American friend is a symbol for the way the American plantation owners are taking over Macondo. When Meme, a descendant of the town's founders, begins to learn English, the foreigners' encroachment on Macondo's culture becomes obvious. The concrete threat posed by the encyclopedia is later lessened when Aureliano Segundo uses it to tell his children stories. Because he does not speak English, Aureliano Segundo makes up stories to go with the pictures. By creating the possibility for multiple interpretations of the text, he unwittingly diffuses the encyclopedia's danger.

The Golden Chamber Pot

The golden chamber pot that Fernanda del Carpio brings to Macondo from her home is, for her, a marker of her lofty status; she believes that she was destined to be a queen. But while the gold of the chamber pot is associated with royalty, the function of the chamber pot is, of course, associated with defecation: a sign of the real value of Fernanda's snooty condescension. Later, when José Arcadio (II) tries to sell the chamber pot, he finds that it is not really solid gold, but, rather, gold-plated. Again, this revelation represents the hollowness of Fernanda's pride and the flimsiness of cheap cover-ups.

大英百科全书

梅梅从她的美国朋友那里收到了一本大英百科全书。这首先在小说中起到了一个象征的作用,象征着美国种植园主正在吞噬马贡多小镇。当梅梅,这个马贡多创建者的后代,开始学习英语的时候,标志着外国殖民者对马贡多的文化侵蚀开始公开化。后来当奥雷良诺·塞贡多用它来给他的孩子们讲故事的时候,大英百科全书的实际威胁才逐渐减弱。原因是奥雷良诺·塞贡多不会讲英语,他只能依靠大英百科全书中的插图来给孩子们编造故事。奥雷良诺·塞贡多对大英百科全书文本的臆断产生了多重歧义的可能性,无意间削弱了百科全书带来的威胁。

金便盆

对于菲兰达·德卡皮奥来说,这个她从娘家带到马贡多的金便盆是她高贵社会地位的象征。她相信她命中注定要成为女王。这个便盆是用金子做的,象征着王权,但是它的功能却使人自然而然地联想到污秽,而这正是菲兰达的真实写照———傲慢虚伪。后来,当霍塞·阿卡迪奥第二想要卖掉这个便盆时,发现它不是纯金的,而是镀金的。这一发现再次揭露了菲兰达傲慢的虚伪性以及她在肤浅掩饰下的脆弱性。

SUMMARY & ANALYSIS

Chapters 1-2

Summary: Chapter 1

> At that time Macondo was a village of twenty adobe houses...the world was so recent that many things lacked names...
> (See QUOTATIONS, p.154)

One Hundred Years of Solitude begins as a flashback, with Colonel Aureliano Buendía recollecting the years immediately following the founding of Macondo, when a band of gypsies frequently bring technological marvels to the dreamy, isolated village. José Arcadio Buendía, the insatiably curious founder of the town, is obsessed with these magical implements. Using supplies given to him by Melquíades, the leader of the gypsies, he immerses himself in scientific study, to the frustration of his more practical wife, Úrsula Iguarán. Eventually, with Melquíades's prodding, José Arcadio Buendía begins to explore alchemy, the pseudo-science of making gold out of other metals. He is driven by a desire for progress and by an intense search for knowledge that forces him into solitude. Increasingly, he withdraws from human contact, becoming unkempt, antisocial, and interested only in his pursuit of knowledge. But José Arcadio Buendía is not always a solitary scientist. On the contrary, he is the leader who oversaw the building of the village of Macondo, an idyllic place dedicated to hard work and order, filled with young people, and as yet,

断章·取义

第1~2章

综述：第1章

> 当时，马贡多是个20户人家的村庄……这块天地还是新开辟的，许多东西都叫不出名字……
>
> （见第155页引文）

《百年孤独》以倒叙开头，奥雷良诺·布恩地亚上校回想起马贡多刚刚创建的那段时光：一批吉普赛人经常给这个梦幻般与世隔绝的小镇带来一些新奇的技术发明。霍塞·阿卡迪奥·布恩地亚，这个永远无法满足其好奇心的小镇创始人，迷上了这些带有魔力的发明。他利用吉普赛人首领梅尔加德斯提供给他的那些设备从事科学研究。他沉迷于研究之中，达到了乐此不疲的地步，以致他的妻子乌苏拉·伊瓜兰对他感到万念俱灰。与霍塞·阿卡迪奥·布恩地亚相比，乌苏拉·伊瓜兰是一个比较现实的人。后来在梅尔加德斯的引导下，霍塞·阿卡迪奥·布恩地亚开始研究炼金术——一种从其他金属当中提炼金子的伪科学。发明欲望的驱使以及对知识的浓烈兴趣使他陷入了孤独。他逐渐变得独处寡居，衣衫褴褛，憎恶社会，只对探索知识感兴趣。但是霍塞·阿卡迪奥·布恩地亚并不只是一个孤独的科学探索者，相反，他是一个首领。在他的规划下，居民通过勤劳的双手创建了一个田园般的、秩序井然的小镇——马贡多。在这里生活的都是年轻

unvisited by death.

In his quest for knowledge and progress, José Arcadio Buendía's obsession shifts to a desire to establish contact with civilization. He leads an expedition to the north, since he knows there is only swamp to the west and south and mountains to the east. But he then decides that Macondo is surrounded by water and inaccessible to the rest of the world. When he plans to move Macondo to another, more accessible place, however, he is stopped by his wife, who refuses to leave. Thwarted, he turns his attention, finally, to his children: José Arcadio, who has inherited his father's great strength, and Aureliano (later known as Colonel Aureliano Buendía), who seems, even as a child, enigmatic and withdrawn. When the gypsies return, they bring word that Melquíades is dead. Despite his sadness at the news, José Arcadio Buendía does not lose interest in new technology and marvels: when the gypsies show him ice, the patriarch of Macondo proclaims it the greatest invention in the world.

Summary: Chapter 2

In telling the story of Macondo's founding, the book now moves backward in time. The cousins José Arcadio Buendía and Úrsula Iguarán are born in a small village, the great-grandchildren of those surviving Sir Francis Drake's attack on Riohacha. Úrsula is afraid to consummate their marriage, as children of incest were said to have terrible genetic defects. There was precedent for this: two of their relatives gave birth to a child with a pig's tail. But as time passes after their mar-

人,死亡从来没有降临到这个小镇。

在探索知识和寻求发展的过程当中,霍塞·阿卡迪奥·布恩地亚的思想发生了转变,他产生了一种与外界文明建立联系的欲望。因为他知道西面和南面是沼泽地,东面是山,所以他带领一支探险队向北进发。但是他后来很快得出结论:马贡多四面环水,无法与外界建立联系。因此他计划把马贡多搬迁到另外一个四通八达的地方,然而却遭到了妻子的阻挠,因为她拒绝离开这个地方。在受到挫败之后,他最终把注意力转向了他的孩子们:霍塞·阿卡迪奥和奥雷良诺(后来的奥雷良诺·布恩地亚上校)。霍塞·阿卡迪奥继承了父亲体态健壮的特征,而奥雷良诺在年纪尚小的时候就已经显示出其高深莫测、孤僻的性格。当吉普赛人再次来到马贡多的时候,他们带来了梅尔加德斯死亡的消息。尽管这个消息使他感到悲痛,但是霍塞·阿卡迪奥·布恩地亚并没有对新技术和新发明失去兴趣:当吉普赛人向他展示冰块的时候,这个马贡多的首领立刻宣称这是世界上最伟大的发明。

综述:第2章

在讲述创建马贡多小镇的故事过程中,小说开始倒叙过去发生的故事。霍塞·阿卡迪奥·布恩地亚和乌苏拉·伊瓜兰原本是一对表兄妹,他们共同出生在一个小村庄。他们是攻打列奥阿察时幸存下来的弗朗西斯·德拉克爵士的后裔。乌苏拉非常恐惧过夫妻生活,因为她听说乱伦生下来的小孩会有严重的生理缺陷。因为已经有先例证明了这一点:他们的两个亲戚就生

riage, and Úrsula continues to refuse to have sex out of fear of the genetic deformity of their child, the people of the village begin to mock José Arcadio Buendía. When a rival, Prudencio Aguilar, implies that Buendía is impotent, Buendía kills him. Haunted by guilt and the specter of Aguilar, José Arcadio Buendía decides to leave his home. After many months of wandering, they establish the village of Macondo.

On seeing the ice of the gypsies, José Arcadio Buendía remembers his dream of Macondo as a city built with mirror-walls, which he interprets to mean ice. He immerses himself again in his scientific study, this time accompanied by his son Aureliano. Meanwhile, the older son, José Arcadio—still a teenager—is seduced by a local woman, Pilar Ternera, who is attracted to him because of the huge size of his penis. Eventually, he impregnates her. Before their child can be born, however, he meets a young gypsy girl and falls madly in love with her. When the gypsies leave town, José Arcadio joins them. Grief-stricken at the loss of her eldest son, Úrsula tries to follow the gypsies, leaving behind her newborn girl, Amaranta. Five months later, Úrsula returns, having discovered the simple, two-day journey through the swamp that connects Macondo with civilization.

下了一个带有猪尾巴的小孩。由于害怕生出有生理缺陷的畸形儿，乌苏拉在婚后的日子里始终拒绝与丈夫同房，因此村民开始嘲笑霍塞·阿卡迪奥·布恩地亚。当一个在斗鸡比赛中的竞争对手——普鲁登西奥·阿吉廖尔暗示他性无能时，霍塞·阿卡迪奥·布恩地亚将他杀死了。由于杀人负疚感的折磨以及阿吉廖尔鬼魂的纠缠，他决定离开家乡。经过数月的艰苦跋涉，他们建立了马贡多小镇。

见到吉普赛人带来的冰块后，霍塞·阿卡迪奥·布恩地亚回想起当初他创建马贡多的一个梦想——一个用镜子砌成的城市，他把这个梦想中的城市阐释为冰块。他再一次沉浸在科学研究当中，不同的是这一次有儿子奥雷良诺陪伴在他左右。同时，还未成年的大儿子霍塞·阿卡迪奥受到了当地一个女人——皮拉·苔列娜的引诱。皮拉·苔列娜引诱霍塞·阿卡迪奥的原因是因为他的阳物非常巨大。后来霍塞·阿卡迪奥使皮拉·苔列娜怀孕了。然而在孩子出生之前，他碰到了一个吉普赛女孩并且疯狂地爱上了她。当吉普赛人离开马贡多小镇时，霍塞·阿卡迪奥跟随他们流浪去了。大儿子的出走致使乌苏拉悲痛欲绝，她扔下刚出生不久的女儿——阿玛兰塔去寻找吉普赛人的踪迹。五个月过后，乌苏拉回来了，当她路过沼泽地时，她发现了一条连接马贡多与外部文明世界的通道。这个通道非常方便，只需花费两天的行程。

Analysis: Chapters 1-2

One Hundred Years of Solitude does not adopt a straightforward approach to telling its version of history. The progression of time from the town's founding to its demise, from the origins of the Buendía clan to their destruction, provides a rough structure for the novel. But García Márquez does not necessarily tell events in the order that they happen. Rather, flitting forward and backward in time, García Márquez creates the mythic feel and informality of a meandering oral history. Although the first extended episode of the novel tells of the gypsies who come to Macondo bearing technological innovations that seem miraculous to the citizens of the isolated village, the first sentence of the novel refers to an episode far in the future, the planned execution of Colonel Aureliano Buendía. The story of the gypsies, leading up to the moment when José Arcadio Buendía sees ice for the first time, is cast as Colonel Aureliano Buendía's recollection, and so, immediately in the novel, there is a chronological disjunction.

This feeling of befuddled time is compounded by the fact that, at first, we are not sure of *One Hundred Years of Solitude*'s historical setting. At the founding of Macondo, "the world was so recent that many things lacked names," but we also learn that Ursula's great-grandmother was alive when Sir Francis Drake attacked Riohacha, an actual event that took place in 1568. In real life, this perception of time would be impossible. Obviously Sir Francis Drake lived long after the world grew old enough for every object to have a name. Critic Regina Janes points out that these two occurrences are not meant to be an accurate picture of historical events. Instead,

品评:第1~2章

《百年孤独》没有采用平铺直叙的方式来叙述故事。时间的演进,比如从小镇的创建到毁灭、从布恩地亚家族的诞生到毁灭,为小说提供了一个大致的框架。但是加西亚·马尔克斯没有按照事件发生的先后顺序来讲述故事,而是在时间上采用了前后跳跃的方式来讲述一部口述历史。这种创作方式能够产生一种历史的虚构感和非正式性的效果。小说的开头叙述了吉普赛人的故事,吉普赛人给马贡多带来了新发明,而这些新发明对于这个与世隔绝的小镇居民来说简直就是奇迹。值得注意的是,小说的第一句话涉及了一个远在将来才会发生的情节——奥雷良诺·布恩地亚上校的行刑。同时,奥雷良诺·布恩地亚上校对吉普赛人的回忆进而又涉及到了霍塞·阿卡迪奥·布恩地亚第一次见到冰块的那一时刻,这样一来,小说的叙事顺序在瞬刻间被打乱了。

由于我们无法确定《百年孤独》小说发生的历史背景,这一事实又增添了时间上错乱的感觉。在马贡多小镇创建之初,"世界是如此之新,以致许多事物还未被命名,"但是我们知道乌苏拉的曾祖母在弗朗西斯·德拉克爵士攻打列奥阿察(1568年发生的真实历史事件)时还活着。按照推算,这个时间在现实是无法成立的。很显然,远在弗朗西斯·德拉克爵士生活的时代,世界历史有足够的时间给所有的事物命名。批评家雷吉娜·简指出,这两种事件的发生并不意味着我们有必要再现历史事件的真实场景。相反,加西亚·马

65

the disjunction between them allows García Márquez to disorient us, getting us thoroughly lost in the murky historical swamp in which he has placed us.

This strangely indefinite chronological framework blurs the distinctions between memory, history, and fiction. The arrival of the gypsies in town is framed as Colonel Aureliano Buendía's memory rather than as an authoritative reframing of history. As a memory, it assumes subjective and dreamlike qualities that are supposed to be absent from textbook history. This is a narrative strategy that is evident throughout the novel—memory is given the same authority as history, and history is subject to the same emotional colorings and flights of fancy as memory. When, much later in the novel, the inhabitants of the town forget about the massacre of the banana workers, their amnesia constitutes an actual erasing of history. In *One Hundred Years of Solitude*, reality assumes the qualities of human fantasy and memory, and time itself is subject to the same distortions. People in this novel live for impossibly long periods of time, and rain descends for years without stopping; on the other hand, years sometimes pass by without mention or notice from the narrator. The extreme subjectivity of experienced reality is one of the themes of this novel. It is the human tendency toward the fantastic and the absurd that shapes our version of reality: magical realism, then, merely captures a version of reality colored by myth and memory, by human fantasy, and by our own subjectivity.

While we observe that the novel begins with a historical disjunction, however, it is important to note that *One Hundred Years of Solitude* is deliberately structured to trace a very definite narrative, one of epic—or perhaps biblical—proportions.

尔克斯利用时间上的错乱来迷惑我们，他使读者彻底地迷失在模糊的历史沼泽之中。

这种奇特的、颠倒时间次序的叙事结构模糊了记忆、历史以及幻想之间的界限。吉普赛人的到来是在奥雷良诺·布恩地亚上校记忆中产生的，而不是史实的再现。记忆具有主观、幻想的特征，这种特征可以脱离小说历史而存在。这就是整部小说所采用的、具有明显特征的叙事策略：记忆被赋予历史的权威性，而历史被赋予了只有记忆才具有的情感色彩以及联发出来的想象力。在小说的后面情节里，小镇居民忘记了香蕉工人大屠杀事件，这说明他们的健忘真正抹杀了历史。在《百年孤独》小说中，现实呈现出人类幻想和记忆的特征，而且时间常常显得变幻莫测。比如小说中的人物超越了寿命的界限，绵延不断的大雨下了许多年。但从另外一角度来看，时间有时在叙述者没有任何提及的情况下瞬间即逝。现实经历的极端主观性是本小说的主题之一。人类倾向于幻想和制造荒谬，并且依靠幻想和荒谬来塑造现实。那么魔幻现实主义正是运用神话、记忆、幻想以及主观性来捕捉现实的。

我们观察到，小说一开始在时间上的叙事顺序即呈脱节状态，然而值得我们注意的是《百年孤独》小说是有意安排这种结构来进行确定的描述，并模仿史诗——甚至是圣经的叙事方式。正如批评家哈罗德·

The novel is indeed, as the critic Harold Bloom has observed, the Bible of Macondo, and, again, at the very beginning of the novel, just as in the Bible, many things have yet to be named. *One Hundred Years of Solitude* can be seen as a parable for the human quest for knowledge, expressed through the struggles of José Arcadio Buendía—the archetypal man—and his descendents. In the Bible, Adam's job is to name the animals, exercising his power over them and cataloguing them to conform to his vision of the world. In establishing Macondo, José Arcadio Buendía does the same thing. Adam and Eve were expelled from Eden for eating from the Tree of Knowledge, and this novel conveys the same cautionary tale. José Arcadio Buendía's relentless pursuit of knowledge, arguably, drives him to foolishness and eventual insanity. It should not be forgotten that, in his madness, he is tied to a tree that functions as a clear symbol for the Tree of Knowledge, whose fruit tempted Adam and Eve to their original fall.

García Márquez's style of writing is commonly referred to as magical realism, which describes, among other things, the way historical events are colored by subjectivity and memory is given the same weight as history. One easily identifiable trait of magical realism is the way in which mundane, everyday things are mingled with extraordinarily wonderful, or even supernatural, things. In Chapter 2, as José Arcadio is seduced by Pilar Ternera, we learn that "he could no longer resist the glacial rumbling of his kidneys and the air of his intestines, and the bewildered anxiety to flee and at the same time stay forever in that exasperated silence and that fearful solitude." Here, García Márquez describes very specific physical events side by side with huge, abstract emotions. This is typical of

布卢姆指出,该小说的确是一部马贡多的圣经。与圣经相似的是,在小说的开篇,许多事物还没有被命名。《百年孤独》小说可以视作一部人类探索知识的寓言,这种探索的精神体现在以霍塞·阿卡迪奥·布恩地亚为代表的人物及其后代的身上。在圣经里,亚当的使命就是给动物命名并对它们发号施令,而且按照自己的世界观来对动物进行分门别类。在创建马贡多的时候,霍塞·阿卡迪奥·布恩地亚的所作所为与亚当如出一辙。亚当和夏娃因吃了智慧树之果而被逐出伊甸园,这一点在小说中得到了同样的印证。霍塞·阿卡迪奥·布恩地亚对知识执着的追求却使他走向愚昧,甚至最终到了发疯的地步。值得注意的是,霍塞·阿卡迪奥·布恩地亚发疯后被绑在了一棵树上,在这里,这棵树是一个明显的象征,它象征着智慧之树,正是智慧树之果引诱了亚当和夏娃,招致了他们的堕落。

加西亚·马尔克斯的写作风格被普遍认同为魔幻现实主义。魔幻现实主义运用主观性和记忆的方式来刻画历史事件,取得了与历史史实同等重要的效果。魔幻现实主义的一个显著特征就是把世俗的、日常生活发生的事件与异乎寻常的,甚至超自然的现象结合起来进行艺术的再加工。在小说第二章,当霍塞·阿卡迪奥被皮拉·苔列娜引诱后,我们看到:"他再也无法抵制肾脏发出雪崩般的轰鸣。空气在他肠子中蠕动,不知所措的焦虑不仅致使他想逃离,同时又使他沉浸在易怒的情绪和恐惧的孤独之中。"在这里,加西亚·

magical realism: just as the distinctions between different times are muddled up, the distinction between the real and the magical, or between the ordinary and the sublime, become confused.

Chapters 3-4

Summary: Chapter 3

As a result of Úrsula Iguarán's discovery of a route connecting Macondo with civilization, the village begins to change. The village grows along with the Buendía family, with José Arcadio Buendía playing a key role in the expansion of both. Pilar Ternera gives birth to the son of the missing José Arcadio. The boy is named Arcadio. Joining the family, too, is an orphan girl, Rebeca, who arrives mysteriously one day and whose origin is unclear. Nevertheless, the Buendías raise her as one of their own children, first conquering her self-destructive habits of eating dirt and whitewash. Rebeca, it soon becomes evident, is afflicted with an insomnia that also causes memory loss. Eventually, the entire town becomes infected with insomnia and the associated amnesia. To facilitate memory, the inhabitants of the town begin to label everything; First they put up a giant sign to remind themselves that god exists, and then dread the day when the labels will have no meaning because the residents will have forgotten how to read. Pilar Ternera, who tells fortunes on a deck of cards, now uses the cards to tell the past as well. The insomnia is only cured when, unexpectedly, Melquíades the gypsy returns to town bearing an antidote. Melquíades, who, it seems, has returned from the dead, brings with him a technology never before seen

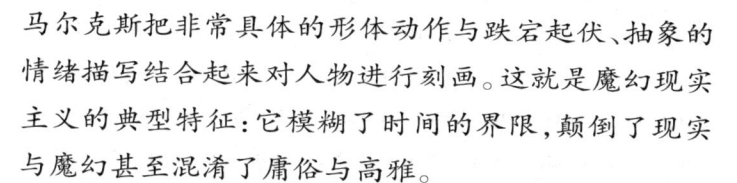

马尔克斯把非常具体的形体动作与跌宕起伏、抽象的情绪描写结合起来对人物进行刻画。这就是魔幻现实主义的典型特征：它模糊了时间的界限，颠倒了现实与魔幻甚至混淆了庸俗与高雅。

第3~4章

综述：第3章

乌苏拉·伊瓜兰发现了一条连接马贡多小镇与文明世界的通道，小镇由此开始发生了变化。小镇逐渐发展起来了，布恩地亚家族也随之壮大，其中老霍塞·阿卡迪奥·布恩地亚功不可没。皮拉·苔列娜为失踪的霍塞·阿卡迪奥生下了一个儿子，名叫阿卡迪奥。孤女蕾贝卡也加入了这个大家庭。她的到来很神秘，而且身世并不为人所知。无论如何，布恩地亚家族还是收养了她，并把她当作自家的孩子抚养，还改正了她吃土和白墙灰的自残习惯。然而不久，蕾贝卡明显地受到了失眠的折磨，并且失去了记忆。最终整个小镇也逐渐地被传染上了失眠症，并且引发了健忘症。为了帮助记忆，小镇居民开始给每一件东西都贴上标签。起先他们竖起一个巨大的标示牌，以便提醒他们上帝是存在的。后来他们日益感到恐惧，因为他们担心会忘记如何去认字，所以标签也就显得毫无意义。皮拉·苔列娜用一副扑克牌占卜未来，现在用它来告知过去。出乎人们预料的是，失眠症居然被回到小镇的吉普赛人梅尔加德斯带来的解毒药治好了。梅尔加德斯

in Macondo, the daguerreotype; José Arcadio Buendía sets to work trying to make a daguerreotype of God, to prove His existence. Aureliano, José Arcadio Buendía's second son, has become a master silversmith. He spends his days shut up in the laboratory that he shares with Melquíades, each of them obsessively absorbed with their strange pursuits. Now mature, Aureliano remains solitary and aloof, apparently uninterested in women.

As the family and village expand, Úrsula vastly expands the Buendía house. The town magistrate, a representative of the central government newly arrived in the formerly autonomous Macondo, attempts to dictate the color their house will be painted. José Arcadio Buendía drives the magistrate, Don Apolinar Moscote, out of town, and when Moscote returns—accompanied by his family and several soldiers—Buendía forces him to forfeit much of his authority over the village. Despite his father's enmity toward the magistrate, however, Aureliano falls in love with the magistrate's youngest daughter, Remedios Moscote.

Summary: Chapter 4

Lonely and despairing, Aureliano sleeps with Pilar Ternera, the same woman whom his older brother had impregnated, and she helps Aureliano in his campaign to marry Remedios. While Aureliano is pining over the impossibly young Remedios, the Buendía family's two girls—Amaranta and the adoptee Rebeca—both fall in love with a stranger, Pietro

似乎死而复生,他此次带来了马贡多居民从未见识过的一种新技术:银板照相术。霍塞·阿卡迪奥·布恩地亚立刻付诸于行动,千方百计地想拍摄一张上帝的照片,以便证明上帝的存在。霍塞·阿卡迪奥·布恩地亚的二儿子奥雷良诺这时已成为了一个手艺精湛的银器匠。他和梅尔加德斯一样,整天把自己关进试验室,各自沉浸在他们怪异的探索之中。奥雷良诺现在已经是一个成熟的男人了,但他总是孤身一人,离群索居,显然对女人一点都不感兴趣。

随着家族的兴旺以及小镇的扩大,乌苏拉扩建了家族的宅邸。这时,一位自称代表中央政府的行政长官来到了这个原先自治的小镇马贡多,企图命令居民按照他规定的颜色来粉刷房屋。霍塞·阿卡迪奥·布恩地亚一怒之下把这个名字叫做唐·阿波利纳尔·摩丝柯特的行政长官逐出了马贡多。然而不久摩丝柯特又带领着家眷和几名士兵返回到了马贡多,而霍塞·阿卡迪奥·布恩地亚迫使他放弃了统治马贡多的大部分权力。尽管父亲对行政长官抱有敌意,然而奥雷良诺还是爱上了行政长官的小女儿——蕾麦黛丝·摩丝柯特。

综述:第4章

由于倍感孤独和绝望,奥雷良诺投入了皮拉·苔列娜的怀抱,就是他的哥哥曾经使之受孕的女人。就是这个女人帮助他出谋划策,以迎娶蕾麦黛斯。就在奥雷良诺痛苦追求年龄尚小、还不可能成为他妻子的蕾麦黛丝之时,布恩地亚家族的两个女儿——阿玛兰

ONE HUNDRED YEARS OF SOLITUDE

Crespi, who has come to Macondo to install a pianola in the Buendía house. They make themselves sick with love: Rebeca goes back to eating earth and whitewash, and Crespi decides he wants to marry her. The marriages—of Rebeca to Crespi and Aureliano to Remedios—are arranged, even though Amaranta, wildly jealous of Rebeca, vows to stop her marriage.

When the gypsy Melquíades slowly passes away, he is the first person to die in Macondo. After his mourning period is over, a semblance of happiness descends on the house: Pietro Crespi and Rebeca are in love, courting, and Aureliano is becoming closer to his future bride, Remedios. Even the news that Pilar Ternera is pregnant with his child does not bother Aureliano. But the happiness does not last. Amaranta's threat to destroy Rebeca's wedding deeply troubles Rebeca. José Arcadio Buendía, exhausted by his endless research into the unknown, slips into insanity. He has visions of the man he killed early in his life and is wracked with sorrow over the solitude of death. He becomes convinced that the same day is repeating itself over and over again. He begins to rage, tearing up the house, and it takes twenty men to drag him out and tie him to a tree in the backyard, where he remains until the end of his life, many years later.

Analysis: Chapters 3-4

It might be said that Macondo's evolution is a parable, evocative of the typical arc of human societal progress, and that

塔和养女蕾贝卡共同爱上了一个来到马贡多、给她们家里安装自动钢琴的陌生人——皮埃特罗·克列斯比。她们共同患上了相思病。蕾贝卡吃土和白墙灰的老毛病又犯了,而克列斯比做出决定,准备娶她为妻。尽管阿玛兰塔对蕾贝卡的嫉妒发展到了丧心病狂的地步,并且发誓要阻止她与克列斯比结婚,但是蕾贝卡与克列斯比以及奥雷良诺与蕾麦黛斯的婚事已被安排妥当。

吉普赛人梅尔加德斯慢慢地死去了,他是马贡多第一个死亡的人。梅尔加德斯的丧期刚过,一种表面上的幸福降临到布恩地亚家族:皮埃特罗·克列斯比和蕾贝卡恋爱了;经过努力的追求,奥雷良诺与他的准新娘——蕾麦黛斯变得更加亲密了,甚至连皮拉·苔列娜怀上他的孩子的消息都没有影响到他。但是这种幸福并没有延续多久,阿玛兰塔企图破坏蕾贝卡与克列斯比的婚姻,这种威胁深深地困扰着蕾贝卡。厌倦了对未知领域永无止境的探索,疲惫不堪的老布恩地亚精神错乱了。他看见了他年轻时杀死的那个人的鬼魂。由于他对死亡产生了过度的悲伤,他被彻底地击垮了。他认为同一天在永无止境地重复着,因此他开始暴怒,捣毁房屋。最后花费了20个人的力气才把他从屋里拖出来,然后把他捆绑在后院的一棵树上。他就被绑在那里度过了许多年,直到生命的终结。

品评:第3~4章

可以说马贡多的发展史是一部寓言,它典型地再现了人类社会发展的轨迹。马贡多小镇是所有人类文

the village is a microcosm for all of human civilization. In this section, the technological and social changes that accompany modernization cause the society to become more cosmopolitan, containing both greater wealth and greater social problems than Macondo did in its earlier state. Increased traffic through the town brings prosperity, but it also brings some of the horrors associated with capitalism. For example, Aureliano stumbles into a tent where a girl is being forced to sleep with many men consecutively—it will take seventy a night, for ten more years, to pay off her family's debts. The town is also changed by governmental interference that contact with the outside world allows. José Aureliano Buendía has his first encounter in this section with the civil authorities that will increasingly seize control of the town. Gradually, it is suggested, so-called progress brings loss of innocence and potential sources of conflict.

But the changes happening to the city go beyond a simple allegory of political change in world history. The conflict between José Arcadio Buendía's style of government and the regulations brought in by the magistrate reflects a political agenda that is very specific to García Márquez and Latin America. García Márquez is well known as a friend of Fidel Castro, a Communist, and revolutionary sympathizer. José Arcadio Buendía's Macondo is a utopian portrait of what an ideally communist society might be like. He has mapped out the city so that every house has equal access to water and shade, and he tells the magistrate that "in this town we do not give orders with pieces of paper." Later on, we will see that this early utopia cannot last, and Macondo will become embroiled in a revolution against a harshly regulatory government. If

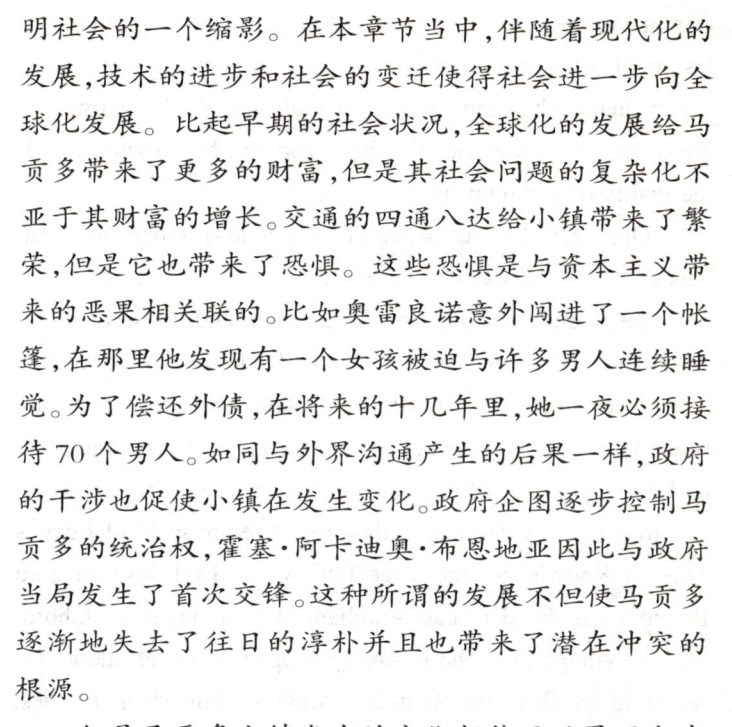

明社会的一个缩影。在本章节当中,伴随着现代化的发展,技术的进步和社会的变迁使得社会进一步向全球化发展。比起早期的社会状况,全球化的发展给马贡多带来了更多的财富,但是其社会问题的复杂化不亚于其财富的增长。交通的四通八达给小镇带来了繁荣,但是它也带来了恐惧。这些恐惧是与资本主义带来的恶果相关联的。比如奥雷良诺意外闯进了一个帐篷,在那里他发现有一个女孩被迫与许多男人连续睡觉。为了偿还外债,在将来的十几年里,她一夜必须接待70个男人。如同与外界沟通产生的后果一样,政府的干涉也促使小镇在发生变化。政府企图逐步控制马贡多的统治权,霍塞·阿卡迪奥·布恩地亚因此与政府当局发生了首次交锋。这种所谓的发展不但使马贡多逐渐地失去了往日的淳朴并且也带来了潜在冲突的根源。

但是马贡多小镇发生的变化超越了世界历史中一个简单政治变革的寓言。霍塞·阿卡迪奥·布恩地亚的统治方式与政府行政长官带来的法律之间发生的冲突反映了一个政治议题,这种政治议题对于加西亚·马尔克斯和拉丁美洲来说具有非常切身的感受。众所周知,加西亚·马尔克斯是费德罗·卡斯特罗——一个共产主义者——的朋友,还是革命的支持者。霍塞·阿卡迪奥·布恩地亚统治下的马贡多是一个理想的共产主义者所向往的、乌托邦式的社会。他预先制定好马贡多的城镇规划,以便每家每户走同样的距离去汲水,每一间屋子都能享有同样多的阳光。他警告行政长官:"在这个镇里,我们不凭纸张发号施令。"接

García Márquez appears to support an idealistically communist vision of what society should be like, his strong reaction against dictatorship and oppression indicates his disapproval of the oppressive tendencies that have come to be associated with the reality of communism.

One way the residents of Macondo respond to these changes is by embracing solitude more and more. In this section, the Buendías—José Arcadio Buendía and his second son, Aureliano—first begin to turn away from society, to devote themselves single-mindedly to their crafts and intellectual pursuits. José Arcadio Buendía goes insane, his mind crumbling under the pressure of his solitary musings, and he has to be tied to a tree. Symbolically, this tree is reminiscent of Eden's Tree of Knowledge, the same tree whose fruit José Arcadio Buendía has dared to eat. Aureliano's solitude seems inborn: like the village itself, he is simply happier when left alone. He seems to feel love for Remedios Moscote, but when she dies, later in the book, he feels no great sorrow. Emotions seem beyond him, as do relationships, and he is fundamentally detached from people and feelings. It will be revealed throughout the novel that this is the curse of much of the Buendía family, whose intensity of emotion and inwardness cannot accommodate social interaction. Those family members who are not solitary and hermetic, of course—like Aureliano Segundo—are radical extroverts. One of the complexities of *One Hundred Years of Solitude* is that even as the narrator treats the story very seriously and realistically, he also points out morals

下来我们看到,这种早期乌托邦式的生活再也无法继续下去,因为马贡多即将卷入一场反抗政府残酷统治的革命。如果说加西亚·马尔克斯认同共产主义者理想式的世界观,但他对专政和压迫的强烈抗议却表明他并不赞同共产主义在现实世界里的专制统治。

马贡多居民对变化的反应之一就是在孤独中躲避。在本章节当中,布恩地亚家族中的霍塞·阿卡迪奥·布恩地亚和他的二儿子——奥雷良诺一开始先把自己与社会隔绝开来,然后专心致志地投入到知识的探索和手工艺品的制作之中。然而霍塞·阿卡迪奥·布恩地亚却发疯了,他在孤独中苦思冥想,沉重的思想负担导致他的精神崩溃了,以致于人们必须把他捆绑在一棵树上。这棵树具有象征意义,使人联想起伊甸园中的智慧树,霍塞·阿卡迪奥·布恩地亚也敢于品尝伊甸园中的智慧树之果。奥雷良诺的孤独性格似乎与生俱来,就像马贡多小镇与世隔绝的状态一样,当他一个人独处一隅的时候反而觉得更加愉快。他感觉到他爱上了蕾麦黛丝·摩丝柯特,但是当蕾麦黛丝·摩丝柯特后来去世时,他并没有感觉到巨大的悲痛。他似乎既无感情,又无友情,他从根本上与人和感情隔绝了。这就是整部小说揭示出来的、布恩地亚家族衰亡的主要内因:缺失的情感,内向的性格显然无法形成与社会的交流。当然,布恩地亚家族里也有不孤独,不固步自封的家庭成员,比如奥雷良诺·塞贡多,他们反倒是极端外向的人。《百年孤独》小说的复杂性之一就在于:虽然叙述者往往采用非常严肃的态度和现实的手法来叙述故事,但是有时也会借助道德,甚至寓言

in the narrative, sometimes treating it like a fable. What is suggested in the fable of the solitary Buendías is perhaps that human society is fundamentally polarizing and perhaps ultimately unfulfilling. Man is uncomfortable in society, and—as Aureliano and then José Arcadio Segundo discover—when he is alone, he may find comfort, but no great joy.

The reference in Chapter 4 to Big Mama's funeral, which will happen more than a hundred years after Melquíades is buried, reflects another aspect of Márquez's body of work: its intertextuality and web of connections among many of his short stories and novels. Though only touched on in *One Hundred Years of Solitude*, this funeral is the subject of a short story by García Márquez entitled "Big Mama's Funeral." Although it was published in 1962, five years before *One Hundred Years of Solitude*, "Big Mama's Funeral" mentions Colonel Aureliano Buendía and his war. Macondo is also mentioned in a number of other García Márquez stories, including his early work, *Leaf Storm*. These crossovers give García Márquez's body of work an almost mythical status; he has created not just a fiction, but a mythology of place and history.

Chapters 5-6

Summary: Chapter 5

Soon after Remedios reaches puberty, she and Aureliano are married (Rebeca's wedding, which is to take place at the

来讲述故事。孤独的布恩地亚家族在寓言中呈现出这样的一种寓意：人类社会正在从根本上走向极端，最终将会导致自我毁灭。如同奥雷良诺以及后来的霍塞·阿卡迪奥·塞贡多所感悟到的那样，人在社会中是局促不安的，只有在孤独中才能找到一份安逸，但是但是没有大的快乐。

在第四章，小说提到"大妈的葬礼"。其实大妈的葬礼是在梅尔加德斯死后100多年后才发生的事情。这种所指反映了马尔克斯作品的另一个层面：互文性以及他的许多短篇小说与长篇小说之间相互交织的关系网。虽然这种指涉在《百年孤独》小说中只是点到为止，但是这场葬礼却是加西亚·马尔克斯另一部短篇小说——《大妈的葬礼》的主题。尽管这部短篇小说发表于1962年，比《百年孤独》早出版5年之久，但是作者在《大妈的葬礼》中提到了奥雷良诺·布恩地亚上校以及有关他的战争。马贡多小镇也在加西亚·马尔克斯的其他几部小说中出现过，其中就包括他的早期作品《落叶纷飞》。这种交叉式的叙述方式给加西亚·马尔克斯的作品赋予了魔幻色彩；他不仅创作了一部小说，而且在历史的空间中创造了一个神话。

第5~6章

综述：第5章

蕾麦黛丝一到青春期，她就和奥雷良诺结了婚（蕾贝卡的婚事本应在同期举办，但因皮埃特罗·克列

same time, is postponed because Pietro Crespi is called away by an urgent letter that says his mother is gravely ill. The letter proves false, and Amaranta is suspected of forging it to delay the marriage). Remedios provides a breath of fresh air in the Buendía household, endearing herself to everybody and even deciding to raise Aureliano's bastard son—born to Pilar Ternera—as her own child. He is named Aureliano José. Soon after the marriage, however, Remedios dies of a sudden internal ailment, possibly a miscarriage, and the house plunges into mourning. This period of grief proves yet another in the interminable set of obstacles for Rebeca and Pietro Crespi, who cannot be married while the Buendía household is in mourning. Another setback is the tremendously long time it takes to build the first church in Macondo, which has been visited for the first time by organized religion. The priest who is building the church makes the startling discovery that José Arcadio Buendía's apparent madness is not as severe as everyone thinks. The gibberish he spouts is not nonsense, but pure Latin in which he can converse.

The period of mourning and delay are simultaneously brought to an end by the return of José Arcadio, the oldest son of José Arcadio Buendía. He is a beast of a man—enormously strong, tattooed all over his body, impulsive, and crude. Despite her engagement to Pietro Crespi, Rebeca is enthralled by José Arcadio's masculinity, and they begin a torrid affair, governed by lust. The affair ends in marriage, and they are

斯比的突然离开而意外地被推迟了。原因是皮埃特罗·克列斯比收到了一封告知他母亲身患重病的紧急信件。这封信后来被证明是一封假信。阿玛兰塔受到了怀疑，人们猜测她为了拖延蕾贝卡的婚事而伪造了这封假信）。蕾麦黛丝为布恩地亚家族注入了一股清新的空气，并且受到每个人的喜爱。她甚至决定把奥雷良诺的私生子（由皮拉·苔列娜所生）当作自己的孩子来抚养。这个孩子被取名为奥雷良诺·霍塞。然而婚后不久，蕾麦黛丝突然死于疾病，可能是小产的原因。蕾麦黛丝的去世使整个家族顿时陷入了悲痛之中。哀悼期的到来对于本来就阻碍不断的蕾贝卡和皮埃特罗·克列斯比来说无疑是雪上加霜——他们无法在哀悼期里完婚。另外一个不幸就是建设教堂的工期显得遥遥无期。这个处于建设中的教堂即将成为马贡多的第一个教堂，有组织的正统教会首次造访了马贡多。负责建设教堂的牧师惊人地发现：霍塞·阿卡迪奥·布恩地亚的疯病并没有人们预料的那样严重。通过对话，他发现霍塞·阿卡迪奥·布恩地亚满嘴胡言的并非什么鬼话，而是纯正的拉丁语。

霍塞·阿卡迪奥·布恩地亚的长子霍塞·阿卡迪奥的归来使得哀悼期和蕾贝卡延期的婚事同时终止了。返回家乡的霍塞·阿卡迪奥简直像一头野兽，他健壮无比、浑身刺青、异常冲动而且非常粗鲁。尽管蕾贝卡已经与皮埃特罗·克列斯比订了婚，但是她还是被霍塞·阿卡迪奥的男性气魄迷住了。强烈的欲望驱使他们开始疯狂地偷情。最终他们的偷情以结婚而告终，但是他们被怒不可遏的乌苏拉逐出了家门。然而皮埃

exiled from the house by the outraged Úrsula. There develops, however, a growing tenderness between Crespi and Amaranta, whom he had previously spurned in favor of Rebeca.

Aureliano, who had resigned himself to solitude after the death of Remedios, soon finds a larger concern: the impending war between the Conservative government—represented in Ma-condo by the magistrate who is Aureliano's father-in-law, Don Apolinar Moscote—and the insurgent Liberals. Upset by the dishonesty and corruption of the Conservatives, Aureliano allies himself with the Liberals. When war breaks out and the town is brutally occupied by the Conservative army, Aureliano leads young men of the town in a rebellion, conquering the town for the Liberals. He leaves at the head of a small Liberal army and is henceforth known in the novel as Colonel Aureliano Buendía. Eventually, he becomes the leader of the Liberal armies.

Summary: Chapter 6

Colonel Aureliano Buendía leaves Macondo with his hastily assembled troops and joins the national civil war effort, fathering seventeen children around the country as he goes. He leaves Arcadio—the illegitimate son of José Arcadio and Pilar Ternera—in charge of the town in his absence, and Ar-ca-dio becomes a dictator, obsessed with order and given to cruelty. When he tries to sleep with Pilar Ternera, his own mother, she sends him a young virgin named Santa Sofía de la Piedad instead. He marries her, and she gives birth to three children: Remedios the Beauty, Aureliano Segundo, and José Arcadio Segundo. When the Liberals lose the war and the Conservatives retake the town, Arcadio is executed by a firing

特罗·克列斯比和阿玛兰塔逐渐变得亲密起来。皮埃特罗·克列斯比曾经拒绝过阿玛兰塔，因为他以前更倾向于喜欢蕾贝卡。

蕾麦黛丝死后，重新陷入孤独的奥雷良诺很快又发现了一个令他更加关注的事件：那就是保守党政府与反叛的自由党分子之间即将爆发的战争。保守党政府在马贡多的代表是行政长官（奥雷良诺的岳父——唐·阿波利纳尔·摩丝柯特）。由于对保守党的欺诈行为和腐败感到忧虑不安，奥雷良诺站到了自由党的一边。当战争爆发，小镇被保守党军队残暴地占领之后，奥雷良诺带领小镇青年奋起反抗，为自由党派夺回了小镇的政权。他带领一小部分自由党部队离开了马贡多，自此以后，他在小说中被称之为奥雷良诺·布恩地亚上校。后来他当上了自由党军队的首领。

综述：第6章

奥雷良诺·布恩地亚上校率领急行军离开了马贡多，加入到了内战当中。他转战南北，沿途一共生了十七个儿子。他把掌管马贡多的权力交给了阿卡迪奥——霍塞·阿卡迪奥与皮拉·苔列娜的私生子，他命令阿卡迪奥在他不在时管理马贡多。然而阿卡迪奥变成了一个独裁者，他滥用权力，残酷地统治着小镇。他欲与皮拉·苔列娜——他的亲生母亲——睡觉，但是皮拉·苔列娜拒绝了他，给他送来一个名叫桑塔·索非亚·德拉佩德的年轻处女。桑塔·索非亚·德拉佩德嫁给了阿卡迪奥并且生了三个孩子：俏姑娘蕾麦黛丝、奥雷良诺·塞贡多和霍塞·阿卡迪奥·塞贡多。当自由

squad. While the war rages, and Arcadio's dictatorship continues, Pietro Crespi proposes marriage to Amaranta, who cruelly rejects him despite her love for him, and he commits suicide. Penitent, she burns her hand horribly, covering it with the black bandage that she will wear until her death.

Analysis: Chapters 5-6

One Hundred Years of Solitude is remarkable for its scope: it is concerned both with events on a grand scale—such as the rebel uprising that begins in this section—and with the minute aspects of its protagonists' lives. It also runs the gamut from the sublime to the disgusting. In one breath, it seems, García Márquez will celebrate the supernatural, and in the next, he will investigate, in great detail, the filthiest of whorehouses. When, in this section, Remedios Moscote reaches puberty, it does not suffice for García Márquez to simply retell the fact: he also produces bloody proof. *One Hundred Years of Solitude* is a novel that, like the prophecies of Melquíades the gypsy, contains everything—the grand and the insignificant, the absurd and the transcendent. In that sense, *One Hundred Years of Solitude* is mimetic: that is, it imitates real life. Real life, of course, includes a seemingly infinite number of voices and a wide array of emotions and qualities. *One Hundred Years of Solitude* gets its epic scope from its attempt to imitate reality, to include everything that life includes. In *One Hundred Years of Solitude*'s attempt at mimesis, too, lies one reason for its confused timeline and tendency to jump from story to story without obvious transition. García Márquez believes that modern life is entropic—chaotic, tending toward eventual dissolution. Thus, he refuses to impose a

党战败,保守党重新占领小镇之后,火枪队对阿卡迪奥执行了死刑。在战争进行到如火如荼之际以及在阿卡迪奥推行暴政期间,皮埃特罗·克列斯比向阿玛兰塔求婚。虽然阿玛兰塔爱皮埃特罗·克列斯比,但她还是残忍地拒绝了他,克列斯比因此自杀了。作为惩罚,阿玛兰塔把自己的一只手严重灼伤,然后用一条黑色的绷带缠在上面。至死她都一直戴着那条黑色的绷带。

品评:第5~6章

《百年孤独》描写的领域非常之广阔:它不仅从宏观的角度叙述了许多重大事件的发生,例如本章一开始就涉及到的反抗起义,还在微观的层面上描绘主人公的生活。有时,小说的描写范围甚至从高雅延伸到了低俗。一会儿,加西亚·马尔克斯似乎倾向于采用超自然力来表达主题思想;另一会儿,在小说文本当中,他又运用非常细腻的描写来刻画妓院的肮脏。在这几章内容当中,当蕾麦黛丝·摩丝柯特进入了青春期,加西亚·马尔克斯并不满足于简单地告知这个事实,他还给出了经血的证据。如同吉普赛人梅尔加德斯的预言一样,《百年孤独》这部小说的内容几乎无所不包:它涵盖了伟大与渺小、荒诞不经与卓越超凡。从这种意义上说,《百年孤独》小说带有模仿性:它模仿现实生活。当然,从表面上看,现实生活包含着无穷无尽的声音、广泛的情感以及生活的品质。《百年孤独》小说试图通过模仿现实来扩展它的创作领域,容纳现实生活中所包含的一切。为了混淆时间的界限,在没有明显过渡的情况下,从一个故事情节跳跃到另一个故事

rigid structure on his novel, choosing instead to allow the novel to meander digressively, at times unraveling, toward the eventual apocalypse at its close.

Despite García Márquez's determination to capture the variety and scope of real life, however, the reader will notice that his language sometimes tends toward the metaphoric and euphemistic rather than the literal and precise. For instance: although García Márquez does not shy away from a narration of the moment when Remedios Moscote first finds menstrual blood in her underwear, he avoids an actual mention of the blood. Instead, he calls it "chocolate-colored paste." And in describing Rebeca's first sex act with José Arcadio, García Márquez refers to her loss of virginity as a loss of "intimacy," a curious circumlocution. These moments leave us asking why García Márquez avoids graphic and realistic use of language throughout the novel in his descriptions of sex and violence and why a novel that explores all aspects of life, both beautiful and disgusting, substitutes euphemisms for a realistic depiction of events. One answer is that García Márquez brings the ordinary world into the realm of the fantastic by using poetic language for mundane things and mundane language for magical events. Another answer might be that García Márquez is attempting, through these circumlocutions, to use language that his characters themselves might use. The novel speaks in Remedios Moscote's voice, describing her blood as she might have. This narrative technique, in which the novel assumes the voice of a character without openly indicating that it is switching perspectives, is known as free indirect discourse. *One Hundred Years of Solitude*'s epic feel can be accounted for by its multiplicity of voices, its desire to see things from different

情节也是小说试图模仿现实的另一个原因。加西亚·马尔克斯认为：现代生活处在一种熵的状态——混乱并将逐步走向消亡。因此在小说中，他拒绝使用僵化的结构。替而代之，他让小说的情节在脱节的状态下曲折发展，有时故意打乱情节，最后以启示作为结尾。

尽管加西亚·马尔克斯试图捕捉现实生活中的多样性和空间的广度，然而读者注意到：相对于平实和精确，他的语言有时更倾向于隐喻和委婉。例如，尽管加西亚·马尔克斯没有回避蕾麦黛丝·摩丝柯特在她内衣上首次发现经血时的描述，但是他避免直接提到"血"字。替而代之，他把血称为"巧克力颜色般的浆糊"。在描写蕾贝卡首次与霍塞·阿卡迪奥发生性行为时，加西亚·马尔克斯把蕾贝卡失去贞操形容为失去了"秘密"，形成了一个有趣的、婉转曲折的表达方法。这时我们不禁会问：在整部小说中，加西亚·马尔克斯为什么避免使用精确、平实的语言来描写性和暴力？为什么一部小说能够描绘一个既美丽壮观又低级庸俗的社会全景图，却用委婉的表达方法来替代现实的描写？一种答案可能是加西亚·马尔克斯运用了诗的语言来描绘世俗的东西，运用世俗的语言来描写魔幻的事件，并以此来把现实的世界带到幻想的领域。另外一个可能的答案是：这些婉转曲折的叙述说明加西亚·马尔克斯试图采用小说中人物角色自身所使用的语言。小说以蕾麦黛丝·摩丝柯特的口吻来描述她的经血。这种叙事技巧被称为自由间接话语，即小说运用主人公的视角来叙述故事，但不公开指出叙事角度的转换。《百年孤独》小说的史诗感基于它叙事的多样

perspectives, and its descriptions of them in the sub-jective terms used by different characters.

It is not just the technological forces of modernization that cause the unraveling of Macondo's utopian, Eden-like community, but the arrival of organized religion in the form of priests and magistrates. Before the priest's arrival, shame is unknown in Macondo—like Adam and Eve before the fall, the citizens are "subject to the natural law" sexually and worship God without a church. Father Nicanor's arrival disturbs that untouched innocence, just as Don Apolinar Moscote's increased power (as he finally succeeds in bringing armed soldiers to help govern Macondo) disturbs the self-governing peace that the town has always enjoyed. Once Macondo's innocence has been lost, efforts to regain it by overthrowing the new leaders only make things worse. For example, Arcadio's revolution against Don Apolinar Moscote's regime only results in worse dictatorship. And, in addition to showing how impossible it is for the town to regain its innocence, Arcadio's dictatorship also shows what can go wrong when well-intentioned governments have cruel leaders and become power-obsessed. This commentary applies outside of the fictional world of *One Hundred Years of Solitude*, criticizing dictatorial regimes in twentieth-century Latin American countries like Cuba and Panama.

Chapters 7-9

Summary: Chapter 7

The Liberals have lost the war, and Colonel Aureliano

性、多角度的叙述以及不同的人物角色的主观性叙事技巧。

与其说马贡多理想式的、伊甸园般的社会是被现代化的技术力量摧毁的,不如说是被以牧师为代表的宗教组织以及行政长官的统治瓦解的。在牧师到来之前的马贡多,羞耻还不为人所知,如同堕落前的亚当和夏娃。居民"根据自然法则"来行事,向上帝祈祷时也不需要教堂。如同唐·阿波利纳尔·摩丝柯特不断膨胀的权利(他曾经带来武装士兵帮助他统治马贡多,他在这方面获得了成功)破坏了小镇一直在享受的和平自治,尼康诺神父的到来玷污了小镇的纯真。一旦失去纯真,为了恢复它而付出努力来推翻新的统治者,反而会使情况变得更糟。比如,奥雷良诺上校向唐·阿波利纳尔·摩丝柯特政权发动的战争换来的只是更加残暴的统治。除了证明恢复小镇的纯真是多么的不可能之外,阿卡迪奥的独裁专政同样向我们展示了这样一个事实:当一个精心策划的政府由一个沉迷于权力的残酷统治者掌管时,将会产生怎样的后果。这个注释超越了《百年孤独》小说虚构的世界,批评了一些拉美国家诸如古巴和巴拿马在20世纪时期的独裁统治。

第7~9章

综述:第7章

自由党人战败后,奥雷良诺·布恩地亚上校和他

Buendía, along with his friend Colonel Gerineldo Márquez, is captured and sentenced to execution by firing squad. His last request is that the sentence be carried out in his hometown of Macondo. He is saved at the final instant, however, by his brother José Arcadio, and, immediately, Colonel Buendía launches another uprising, one of thirty-two he will lead during his military career. He encounters a long string of failures, however, and is abandoned by the Liberal party's official representatives. Eventually, though, he enjoys some success and is able to recapture Macondo and other coastal territory. But an assassination attempt leaves him disillusioned with the constant fighting, and he begins to realize that he is fighting not for ideology but for pride alone. He starts writing poetry again, as he used to do during his courtship with Remedios Moscote.

While Aureliano is fighting his wars, Santa Sofía de la Piedad gives birth to twins fathered by her dead husband, Arcadio; they are named José Arcadio Segundo and Aureliano Segundo. Apart from this happy event, however, tragedy strikes the Buendía family repeatedly. José Arcadio dies mysteriously, and it is unclear whether he has been murdered or has committed suicide. Rebeca, his wife, becomes a hermit, living the rest of her life in solitary grief. Colonel Gerineldo Márquez, who is left in command of the town when Aureliano leaves yet again to fight, has been in love for years with the solitary Amaranta, who spurns him as she did Pietro Crespi. And finally, after years of living outside tied to a tree, José Arcadio Buendía, the patriarch of the clan, dies. A rain of yellow flowers from the sky marks his death.

的朋友格林列尔多·马克斯上校被捕并被判处死刑，将由火枪队执行枪决。奥雷良诺·布恩地亚上校的最后请求就是希望在他的家乡马贡多执行死刑。然而，在最后关头，他被哥哥霍塞·阿卡迪奥救了下来。随后不久，布恩地亚上校又发动另外一场起义——他军事生涯中领导的32场起义之一。然而在遭受了一连串的失败之后，他被自由党的官方代表抛弃了。他后来逐渐取得了一些成功并且有能力再次占领马贡多以及其他一些沿海地区。但是一次暗杀他的行动致使他连年征战的梦想破灭了。他开始意识到他不是为了理想在战斗，而仅仅是出于傲慢而战。他又开始写诗了，恢复了他追求蕾麦黛丝·摩丝柯特期间那种特有的习惯。

在奥雷良诺打仗的期间，桑塔·索非亚·德拉佩德生下了一对双胞胎，孩子们的父亲是她死去的丈夫——阿卡迪奥。他们分别被命名为霍塞·阿卡迪奥·塞贡多和奥雷良诺·塞贡多。在这件喜事之外，悲剧开始不断地降临到布恩地亚家族。霍塞·阿卡迪奥神秘地死亡了，到底是死于谋杀还是自杀，原因始终不得而知。他的妻子——蕾贝卡变成了一个隐居者，在寂寞的忧伤中度过了余生。格林列尔多·马克斯上校此时在奥雷良诺·布恩地亚上校在外打仗期间镇守着马贡多，他与孤独的阿玛兰塔恋爱了多年，但是阿玛兰塔拒绝了格林列尔多·马克斯上校，就像她当年对待皮埃特罗·克列斯比那样。最终，被绑在外面树上度过了多年的霍塞·阿卡迪奥·布恩地亚——这个家族的首领去世了。上天为了哀悼他的死亡，下起了黄花雨。

ONE HUNDRED YEARS OF SOLITUDE

> **Summary: Chapter 8**
>
> *Aureliano José had been destined to find...happiness... but had been directed by a wrong interpretation of the cards.*
> (See QUOTATIONS, p.154)

Time passes, and Aureliano José, the son of Colonel Aureliano Buendía and Pilar Ternera, grows to maturity. He develops an unhealthy passion for his aunt, Amaranta, which she—in her loneliness—comes dangerously close to requiting. The two touch each other and sleep naked together without ever having intercourse. When they are almost discovered kissing, however, Amaranta breaks off the affair, and Aureliano José joins the army. The official Liberal party signs a peace agreement with the Conservative government, an agreement that Colonel Buendía sees as treacherous. He repudiates the agreement and flees the country, and Aureliano José goes with him. While Colonel Aureliano is traveling throughout the Caribbean, starting Liberal uprisings, Macondo settles into relative peace, thriving in its new status as a municipality under the mayor José Raquél Moncada, who is a Conservative but also a humane and intelligent man.

Aureliano José deserts the rebel army and returns home, hoping to marry Amaranta, who continues to avoid him, repelled by the notion of incest. The situation is brought to a tragic close when Aureliano José is killed by a Conservative soldier during an act of civil disobedience. Soon after Aureliano José's desertion, the seventeen sons whom Colonel Aureliano Buendía has fathered over the course of his travels are

综述：第8章

> 奥雷良诺·霍塞注定要……得到幸福……显然不太理解纸牌的预示。
>
> （见第155页引文）

随着时间的流逝，奥雷良诺·布恩地亚上校与皮拉·苔列娜之子——奥雷良诺·霍塞逐渐长大成人了。他对姑妈阿玛兰塔产生了一种病态的恋情。而对于阿玛兰塔来说，出于寂寞难耐，她直到情况发展到了很危险的地步才从这种不健康的恋情中摆脱出来。他们两人相互抚摸而且赤身裸体地睡到一块，但是没有发生性行为。他们的接吻差一点被发现了，阿玛兰塔因此中断了他们之间的恋情，而奥雷良诺·霍塞则参军去了。自由党当局与保守党政府签订了一个和平协议，而这在奥雷良诺·布恩地亚上校看来简直就是一个背信弃义的协议。他拒绝接受协议并且逃离了这个国家，奥雷良诺·霍塞也随他而去了。在布恩地亚上校周游加勒比地区、再次发动自由起义之际，马贡多渡过了一段相对和平的时期。马贡多的局势发生了新的变化，它成立了市政当局，并接受市长——霍塞·拉凯尔·蒙卡达的领导。霍塞·拉凯尔·蒙卡达虽然是保守党分子，但他是一个仁慈而且明智的市长。

奥雷良诺·霍塞叛逃了起义部队返回家乡，他希望与阿玛兰塔结婚。阿玛兰塔受到了乱伦意识的困扰，她坚持避他不见。奥雷良诺·霍塞在一次国内暴乱中被一名保守党士兵枪杀了，他与阿玛兰塔的不伦之恋最终以悲剧收场。奥雷良诺·霍塞叛逃后，奥雷良诺·布恩地亚上校在转战南北之际所生的17个儿子

brought to Macondo to be baptized, and all are given the name Aureliano. Not long after Aureliano José's death, the Colonel himself returns to Macondo as the head of an army. Tall and pale, Colonel Aureliano Buendía has been hardened by his many battles: when a court martial orders that José Raquél Moncada be put to death, he refuses to commute the sentence, despite the longstanding friendship between the two soldiers and the protests of all the town's matriarchs.

Summary: Chapter 9

The execution of Moncada is the beginning of the end. Colonel Gerineldo Márquez, and then Colonel Aureliano Buendía himself, lose faith in the purpose of the war. Gerineldo Márquez devotes himself instead to Amaranta, who steadily rebuffs his protestations of love even as she becomes more and more used to his presence. Withdrawn into himself, Colonel Buendía becomes a shell of a man, unemotional and utterly solitary, without any memories. It is only when Gerineldo Márquez is condemned to death that Colonel Buendía is forced to confront himself, finally acknowledging the emptiness of the war. Together with the freed Colonel Gerineldo Márquez, he fights the bloody battles against his own forces in an effort to convince the Liberals, at last, to end the war. When he signs a peace treaty that he feels represents the Liberal party's failure to uphold their ideals, he thinks that he has betrayed both himself and his party. He attempts suicide but survives the bullet wound in his chest. When Úrsula, his mother, sees that he will live, she makes an effort to rejuvenate the house and to rescue it from the creeping decay that descended

被带到了马贡多并且接受了洗礼,他们都被命名为奥雷良诺。奥雷良诺·霍塞死后不久,布恩地亚上校作为部队的首领返回了马贡多。经历多年征战的布恩地亚上校变得异常冷酷无情,他身体高大、面色苍白。当军事法庭宣布判处格林列尔多·马克斯上校死刑之时,尽管他与格林列尔多·马克斯上校之间还保持着长久的友情,即使全镇的女族长都在抗议,他还是拒绝为格林列尔多·马克斯上校减刑。

综述:第9章

蒙卡达被执行死刑是一个预示最后结果的先兆。格林列尔多·马克斯上校和奥雷良诺·布恩地亚上校先后对战争的目的产生了怀疑。格林列尔多·马克斯一心一意地追求阿玛兰塔。尽管阿玛兰塔越来越习惯于格林列尔多·马克斯总是出现在她的面前,但是她还是坚决地拒绝了他袒露出来的真情。布恩地亚上校得了自闭症,犹如行尸走肉——没有感情、完全地陷入了孤独而且失去了所有的记忆。当格林列尔多·马克斯被判处死刑时,布恩地亚上校这才被迫面对自己,终于感到了战争的空虚。为了最终说服自由党分子结束战争,他和已获自由的格林列尔多·马克斯上校与自己曾经领导过的力量进行了残酷的斗争。当他签订了一个标志着自由党理想幻灭的和平条约时,他认为他同时背叛了自己和自己的政党。他试图自杀,子弹穿透了他的胸膛,但是他侥幸活了下来。当乌苏拉看到布恩地亚上校还能够存活下去的时候,她打算重修宅邸,试图把老宅从战争期间就开始逐渐老化的

on it during the war.

Analysis: Chapters 7–9

This section, describing Colonel Aureliano Buendía's wars and the concurrent changes in Macondo, is one of the most disturbing in the novel. José Aureliano Buendía dies, and even the heavens mourn his passing, miraculously raining down yellow flowers in his memory. Death, in fact, begins to plague the Buendía family: José Arcadio, Arcadio, and Aureliano José all die prematurely and tragically. But perhaps the most troubling of the misfortunes that fill these pages is the dehumanization of Colonel Aureliano Buendía. Once a sensitive man, the Colonel becomes hardened by war, losing his capacity for emotion and even for memory. In *One Hundred Years of Solitude*, miracles like the rain of flowers in honor of José Arcadio Buendía coexist with tragedies, and no mercy is shown to the protagonists.

Throughout *One Hundred Years of Solitude*, the possibility of forgetting the past threatens the coherence of society and relationships. Amnesia strikes Macondo early in the novel, and later, all memory of a massacre is eliminated. Colonel Aureliano Buendía's loss of memory is connected to his inability to experience emotion other than sadness and resignation. The cruel necessities of war have scourged him of any sensitivity and even of the tenderness associated with nostalgic longings for his past. His attempt to commit suicide is not so much a result of shame for having surrendered, one senses, but a way of eliminating his solitary sadness. In *One Hundred Years of*

状态中恢复过来。

品评:第7~9章

这一部分是小说情节中最为高潮迭起的部分之一,描写了奥雷良诺·布恩地亚上校的战争以及马贡多在同一期间发生的变化。霍塞·阿卡迪奥·布恩地亚死了,就连上天也悲悯他的离世,在他的葬礼上奇迹般地下起了黄花雨。事实上,死亡的瘟疫早已开始在布恩地亚家族蔓延:霍塞·阿卡迪奥、阿卡迪奥以及奥雷良诺·霍塞都相继过早而且悲惨地死去了。但是最令人感到困惑不解的也许就是奥雷良诺·布恩地亚上校丧失了人格。经历了战争的洗礼之后,奥雷良诺·布恩地亚上校,这个曾经敏感的人,变得冷酷无情,并且失去了情感的表达能力,甚至记忆的能力。在《百年孤独》小说中,奇迹(比如悼念霍塞·阿卡迪奥·布恩地亚的黄花雨)与悲剧并存而且怜悯也没有眷顾到主人公的身上。

在整部小说中,忘记过去使社会和谐以及人与人之间的关系受到了威胁。在小说情节发展的初期,马贡多小镇曾经染上了健忘症,后来所有有关大屠杀的记忆全部被清除掉了。奥雷良诺·布恩地亚上校丧失记忆的原因与其说是因为他在忧伤中沉沦、顺从于命运的安排,不如说他丧失了体会感情的能力。战争的残酷性顿挫了他的敏感力,甚至泯灭了他渴望回忆过去的天性。他企图自杀并不是因为他对于投降感到耻辱,而是他为了摆脱孤独的悲哀而不得不采取的一种方法。在《百年孤独》小说中,情感滞留于怀旧之中,禁

Solitude, emotion lodges in nostalgia and ties of affection spring from memories of the past. "How awful," Colonel Aureliano Buendía reflects when he returns home after the war, and he finds himself unmoved by seeing his family again and "the way time passes." The fears of change and of the accompanying dulling of emotion are augmented by the fear of memory loss, and Aureliano can barely remember what the past was like. Rebeca, on the other hand, lives her hermit's life accompanied only by memories, which walk "like human beings through the cloistered rooms" and bring her a peace that no actual humans have ever brought to her.

In this section, the novel expands to its largest scope, filled with the most characters; it contains the rebellion and other national political events. The novel seems noisy and crowded at this point, filled with a confusing multiplicity of voices and perspectives. But even as we are overwhelmed by these voices, the Buendías seem to be retreating further and further into solitude. We learn that a deep feeling of alienation lies at the core of Arcadio's obsession with order and his tyranny of the town when he is installed as dictator. Without the ability to connect emotionally with anybody, Colonel Aureliano Buendía retreats into the solitude of his empty mind. Rebeca shuts herself up in her house with memories that take the place of people, and Amaranta refuses all suitors despite her strong desire not to be alone. Úrsula Iguarán, having no one to confide in, talks only to her insane husband, who does not understand her because he now only speaks Latin. Language functions throughout the novel as a barrier between hu-

锢于过去的记忆。战争结束后,当奥雷良诺·布恩地亚上校返回家乡时,他反应道:"多么的可怕啊!"对于久别重逢的家人,他感到无动于衷,叹曰"时间过得真快啊!"记忆丧失的恐惧加剧了奥雷良诺·布恩地亚上校对于变化的担忧,他的情感日渐枯竭,以致他几乎想不起来过去是什么样子了。而另外一方面,蕾贝卡生活在隐居当中,伴随着她的只有记忆。她经常"像一个正常人在与世隔绝的房间里徘徊"。孤独带给她的这份宁静是人类无法真正给予她的。

在这部分内容里,小说描写的范围达到了最广的跨度,也是牵扯人物角色最多的一部分内容;它涉及到了叛乱以及其他国内政治事件。在这几章内容里,小说充满了嘈杂的声音,而且叙事角度繁杂,给人以喧哗与躁动的感觉。尽管我们被这些声音震撼了,但是布恩地亚家族的成员却在这些声音面前退缩,一步步坠入孤独的深渊。我们看到,当阿卡迪奥被任命为小镇的统治者时,一种被异化的感觉深深地植根于他迷恋权力、施行暴政的心底。因为失去了与人交流感情的能力,孤独感侵蚀了奥雷良诺·布恩地亚上校空洞的头脑。蕾贝卡把自己封闭在屋内,沉浸在回忆当中,断绝与人来往;尽管阿玛兰塔抵制孤独的欲望是如此的强烈,但是她还是拒绝了所有追求她的人。乌苏拉·伊瓜兰因找不到倾诉的对象,只能与她发疯的丈夫交谈,但是此时的霍塞·阿卡迪奥·布恩地亚只说拉丁语,因此无法理解妻子的苦衷。贯穿于小说的语言给人与人之间设置了障碍并且把人物置于一个进退两难的境地。这种创作手法的灵感来源于圣经故事

mans, a dilemma inspired by the biblical confusion of Babel.

Not only as individuals, but as a family, too, the Buendías begin to turn in upon themselves. Incest has been bubbling beneath the surface of the story all along: José Arcadio Buendía and Úrsula Iguarán are cousins, and Arcadio wants to sleep with Pilar Ternera, who is his mother. The urge for incest is now at full force as Aureliano José lusts after his lonely aunt, Amaranta, who is tempted by the young man but refuses to sleep with him, horrified by the taboo. This recurring urge, which will reappear again and again among the Buendías, is symptomatic, perhaps, of the family's alienation. They are isolated both in their remote town and by their solitary personalities. And it should be remembered that the act of incest is an essentially repetitive act: relatives who copulate are essentially reproducing and doubling family relationships that already exist. History, for the Buendía family, repeats itself in ever-tightening spirals, drawing the Buendía family inward upon themselves.

Chapters 10–11

Summary: Chapter 10

Colonel Aureliano Buendía has withdrawn even further from society, spending his days locked in his workshop making tiny golden fishes and refusing to speak about politics. Meanwhile, in his adolescence, Aureliano Segundo begins to delve into the esoteric mysteries still preserved in Melquíades'

中"巴别塔"典故的启发。

不仅个人,而且连整个布恩地亚家族都开始闭关自守,断绝了与外界的来往。乱伦的欲望自始至终在故事情节的掩盖下暗潮汹涌:霍塞·阿卡迪奥·布恩地亚和乌苏拉·伊瓜兰夫妻两人原本是表兄妹关系;阿卡迪奥想和他的母亲——皮拉·苔列娜睡觉。奥雷良诺·霍塞对寂寞的姑妈阿玛兰塔产生了恋情,则标志着乱伦的欲望达到了巅峰。阿玛兰塔受到了奥雷良诺·霍塞的诱惑,但是出于对乱伦禁忌的恐惧,她拒绝与他睡觉。这种在布恩地亚家族内不断地循环出现的乱伦欲望也许就是整个家族被异化的一种征兆。处在这个与世隔绝的小镇以及他们孤独的性格是他们被异化的真正原因。值得注意的是,乱伦行为本质上是一种复制的行为:亲属间的乱伦就是再生本身已经存在的家庭关系。对于布恩地亚家族来说,历史不断地在轮回中重演并且导致布恩地亚家族陷入了与世隔绝的状态。

第10~11章

综述:第10章

奥雷良诺·布恩地亚上校越来越脱离现实,他把自己锁在工作间里以制作小金鱼来消磨时光并且拒绝谈论政治。此时,还处在青春期的奥雷良诺·塞贡多开始钻研一些深奥的秘密,这些秘密还保存在梅尔加德斯的试验室里。梅尔加德斯的幽灵时常在他的面前

s laboratory; he is often visited by the specter of Melquíades himself. José Arcadio Segundo—Aureliano Segundo's twin brother—on the other hand, begins to show a religious side. Soon, however, he becomes a cockfighter and sometimes engages in sex with donkeys. The two brothers, who share a strong resemblance until they are fully grown, both start sleeping with the same woman, Petra Cotes, who does not realize that they are not the same man. When Jose Arcadio Segundo is scared off by a venereal disease contracted from Petra Cotes, he ends all contact, while Aureliano Segundo decides to stay with her. The two have a fierce passion for each other, and something magical in their union causes their farm animals to be supernaturally fertile. Soon, Aureliano Segundo becomes fabulously wealthy by virtue of his livestock's productivity. He throws huge parties and engages in colossal displays of wealth. The whole village seems to share in his prosperity.

Driven, like his great-grandfather José Arcadio Buendía, by the impulse to explore, José Arcadio Segundo tries to engineer a navigable river passage to the ocean. He is successful only once in bringing a boat up the river. In his boat are a group of French prostitutes who promote a huge carnival in Macondo. Remedios the Beauty is declared queen of the carnival. She has become the most beautiful woman anyone has ever seen, but still she remains blissfully ignorant and totally innocent, like a child. At the carnival, however, disaster strikes. A rival queen, Fernanda del Carpio, arrives, escorted by mysterious men who begin a riot and then begin firing rifles into the crowd, killing many revelers.

显现。而霍塞·阿卡迪奥·塞贡多(奥雷良诺·塞贡多的双胞胎哥哥)开始对宗教产生了兴趣。但是时隔不久,他变成了一个斗鸡者,甚至有时和驴性交。这两个双胞胎兄弟在他们未成年之前,长相极为相似。兄弟两人同时跟一个叫作佩特娜·柯特的女人睡觉,而佩特娜·柯特并没有意识到他们是两个不同的人。当霍塞·阿卡迪奥·塞贡多从佩特娜·柯特身上染上了性病时,他被吓跑了,彻底中断了与她的往来,但是奥雷良诺·塞贡多决定继续跟她呆在一起。奥雷良诺·塞贡多和佩特娜·柯特彼此之间有着强烈的吸引力,他们的结合产生了一种魔力,这种魔力使他们饲养的牲畜超自然地繁殖。很快,奥雷良诺·塞贡多仅仅依靠牲畜的超自然繁殖力而获得了难以置信的财富。他举办大型的派对,竭力彰显他的富有,一时间整个小镇似乎都在分享他的荣华富贵。

像他的祖父霍塞·阿卡迪奥·布恩地亚一样,探索的冲动力驱使霍塞·阿卡迪奥·塞贡多企图开凿一条通往大海的运河。他获得了仅有一次的成功:沿着运河引来了一艘小船。他的这艘船载来了一群法国妓女,她们在马贡多举办了一场声势浩大的狂欢节。俏姑娘蕾麦黛丝被荣封为狂欢节的女王。俏姑娘蕾麦黛丝是人们曾经见到过的最美丽的女人,但是她却像一个小孩子,保持着幸福的天真,对周围的一切浑然无知。然而灾难突然降临了狂欢节,一个女王竞选者——菲兰达·德卡皮奥在一群神秘人护送下到达狂欢节。这群神秘人引发了暴乱,然后开始向人群开枪,杀死了许多狂欢者。

ONE HUNDRED YEARS OF SOLITUDE

> **Summary: Chapter 11**

The chapter begins by providing us with a history of Fernanda del Carpio. She is raised to believe she is destined for greatness, but her family's wealth has been fading, and her aristocratic line is dying. Upon seeing her at the carnival, Aureliano Segundo becomes obsessed with her, tracking her down in her gloomy city and carrying her home to marry him. Their personalities, however, clash: she is religious and haughty, while he is a devoted hedonist. Scorning his wife's rigid moral and social code, Aureliano Segundo continues to sleep with Petra Cotes, both to ensure the fertility of his animals and because of his wife's prudishness in bed. Meanwhile, Fernanda attempts to transform the once-relaxed Buendía house into a facsimile of her aristocratic home. She rules with an iron hand, and the house becomes rigidly formal and unpleasant. Despite their estrangement, Aureliano Segundo and Fernanda have two children early in their marriage: Renata Remedios (whom everyone calls Meme), and José Arcadio (II). Úrsula, the hundred-year-old matriarch of the clan, says that José Arcadio will become pope.Soon after the birth of Meme, the anniversary of the armistice that ended the civil war occurs, and the president of the Republic tries to honor Colonel Aureliano Buendía with the Order of Merit, which he declines scornfully. His seventeen illegitimate sons, each named Aureliano, arrive at Macondo to celebrate the anniversary, and Aureliano Segundo greets their arrival with revelry, much to Fernanda's consternation. When the seventeen Aurelianos receive the cross of ashes on their foreheads on Ash Wednesday, they do not wash off, and all seventeen brothers

综述：第11章

本章开头向我们讲述了菲兰达·德卡皮奥的家族史。她从小就被灌输：她命中注定要成为一个不凡之人。但是她家道中落，贵族的血脉继承也在逐渐消亡。当奥雷良诺·塞贡多在狂欢节上第一眼看到她时，就即刻被她迷住了。他一路跟踪，在一个阴森的城市里找到了她并把她带回家准备与她结婚。然而他们的性格截然相反：菲兰达·德卡皮奥是一个虔诚的教徒，态度傲慢；而奥雷良诺·塞贡多则是一个好逸恶劳的花花公子。不屑于妻子僵化的道德观念以及墨守成规的社会习俗，奥雷良诺·塞贡多继续与佩特娜·柯特同居。他这样做既可以确保牲畜的繁殖，又可以摆脱妻子一本正经的做爱方式。在此期间，菲兰达·德卡皮奥试图把原本轻松自由的布恩地亚家族变成一个她曾经享受过的贵族式家庭。她运用铁腕手段管理这个家族，使得家庭气氛变得异常凝重，人人郁郁寡欢。尽管奥雷良诺·塞贡多和菲兰达·德卡皮奥彼此疏远，但是他们在结婚不久还是生了两个孩子：蕾纳塔·蕾麦黛丝(人们都叫她梅梅)和霍塞·阿卡迪奥第二。乌苏拉，这个已有百岁老龄的家族女族长，预言霍塞·阿卡迪奥第二将来会成为教皇。梅梅出生后不久，政府举办停战周年纪念活动，共和政府总统极力嘉奖奥雷良诺·布恩地亚上校，准备授予他荣誉勋章，但被后者轻蔑地拒绝了。奥雷良诺·布恩地亚上校的17个都叫作奥雷良诺的私生子来到马贡多庆祝周年纪念，奥雷良诺·塞贡多以盛大的宴会来为他们接风洗尘，这场宴会使菲兰达惊愕不已。在星期三圣灰节仪式上，17个

keep the mark until their deaths. One of the sons, Aureliano Triste, discovers that Rebeca, the widow of José Arcadio Buendía's son José Arcadio, is still living as a hermit in her house. Aureliano Triste and another of the Aurelianos, Aureliano Centeno, decide to remain in Macondo and build an ice factory there, in a sense fulfilling José Arcadio Buendía's early prophecy of a town made of ice. Finally, funded by Aureliano Segundo, Aureliano Triste builds a railroad connection, decisively linking Macondo with the industrial, modern world.

Analysis: Chapters 10-11

Character traits are entirely hereditary in *One Hundred Years of Solitude;* characters are defined largely by how their parents or namesakes behaved. But it appears that the babies in these chapters have been switched at birth: José Arcadio Segundo does not have the size and impulsiveness of his namesake, and Aureliano Segundo is not thin and solitary like the elder man of the same name, Colonel Aureliano Buendía. Instead, José Arcadio Segundo is intense and solitary like the old Colonel, and Aureliano Segundo is given to debauchery and excess, like José Arcadio. With only the names reversed and with such a strong physical resemblance that they are often mistaken for each other, the twins combine the traits of the José Arcadios and the Aurelianos into a single mishmash of

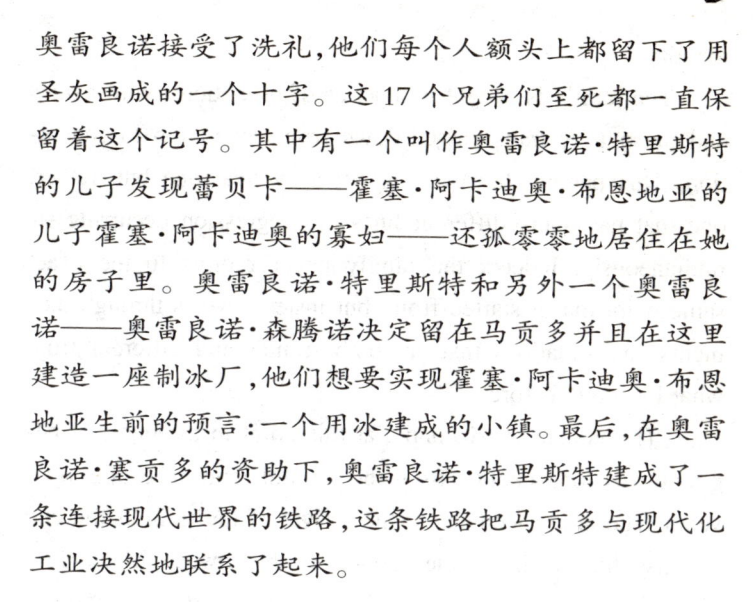

奥雷良诺接受了洗礼,他们每个人额头上都留下了用圣灰画成的一个十字。这 17 个兄弟们至死都一直保留着这个记号。其中有一个叫作奥雷良诺·特里斯特的儿子发现蕾贝卡——霍塞·阿卡迪奥·布恩地亚的儿子霍塞·阿卡迪奥的寡妇——还孤零零地居住在她的房子里。奥雷良诺·特里斯特和另外一个奥雷良诺——奥雷良诺·森腾诺决定留在马贡多并且在这里建造一座制冰厂,他们想要实现霍塞·阿卡迪奥·布恩地亚生前的预言:一个用冰建成的小镇。最后,在奥雷良诺·塞贡多的资助下,奥雷良诺·特里斯特建成了一条连接现代世界的铁路,这条铁路把马贡多与现代化工业决然地联系了起来。

品评:第 10~11 章

在《百年孤独》小说中,人物的性格特征具有完全的继承性;父母的行为举止或者相同名字的称呼基本上决定了各个角色的性格特征。但是在这几章情节里,新生的婴儿好像刚一出世就改变了他们原有的性格特征:霍塞·阿卡迪奥·塞贡多并没有继承与他同名的霍塞·阿卡迪奥所具有的身材魁伟和鲁莽冲动的特征;奥雷良诺·塞贡多也不像与他同名的奥雷良诺·布恩地亚上校那样面容消瘦、性格孤独。相反,霍塞·阿卡迪奥·塞贡多反而像老上校那样性格刚烈、孤独;而奥雷良诺·塞贡多却继承了霍塞·阿卡迪奥浪荡、狂放不羁的性格特征。由于他们颠倒了名字而且身体特征极为相似,因此他们经常被人们误认。这两个双胞胎兄弟把霍塞·阿卡迪奥与奥雷良诺·布恩地亚上校的

identity.

The family is caught in a series of repetitions, with names and personality traits passed down from generation to generation. This pattern, however, is not a cyclical one but, rather, one that has many different lines of progression occurring simultaneously. Indeed, the family never returns to the exact same point that it started from, but instead cycles through moments and situations that are both similar and different from what has gone before.

The village of Macondo, at this point in the book, is beginning its long decline from the blissful innocence of former years. The announcement of the arrival of the train at the end of this chapter shows the sudden clash between Macondo's old-fashioned simplicity and the modern world: the woman who sees the train first describes it as "a kitchen dragging a village behind it!" The modernity that the train introduces to the isolated town brings a period of growth that only serves to mask the decline of the true spirit of the town, the Buendía family. Úrsula Iguarán, whose common-sense wisdom so often proves correct in this novel, realizes it first: "The world is slowly coming to an end and those things [flying carpets and gypsy magic] don't happen here anymore." It is not that marvels do not come to Macondo; indeed, the technology brought by the train is far more miraculous than the magnets and telescopes that the gypsies used to bring. It is instead that the citizens of Macondo are losing their sense of the miraculous, the sense of dreamy wonderment that infused the first pages of *One Hundred Years of Solitude*.

While it is clear that the novel values exuberance and energy, in these chapters it becomes apparent that it rebels a-

性格特征综合成为一个单一的混合体。

布恩地亚家族在轮回中停滞不前。不管是名字还是性格特征都从一代向下一代传承。然而这种轮回并非单一的循环模式,而是许多不同发展线索在同一时间内、同时发生的模式。实际上,布恩地亚家族不是返回到与原来完全一样的起始点,而是在轮回中出现的瞬间时刻和情境与他们原来的经历既相似又有所不同。

在小说中的这一部分情节里,马贡多小镇从它早期幸福、淳朴的生活开始走向长期的衰落。在这一章节的结尾,宣布火车的到来代表了传统守旧、单纯的马贡多与现代文明之间产生的急剧碰撞,第一个看见火车的妇女把它形容为:"好像安了轮子的厨房,后面拖着一个村镇!"火车带来的现代化给与世隔绝的马贡多带来了一段时期的繁荣。而这种繁荣恰恰掩盖了布恩地亚家族本质精神的衰落。在小说中,乌苏拉·伊瓜兰的判断力往往被证明是对的,她第一个意识到:"这个世界正在慢慢地走向末日,而且这些东西(飞毯以及吉普赛人的魔术)再也不会在这儿发生了。"其实,并不是说那些奇迹再也不会在马贡多出现了,而是实际上由火车带来的技术远远比以往吉普赛人带来的那些磁铁和望远镜要神奇的多。由火车带来的技术使马贡多居民丧失了对奇迹和梦想的感觉——那种充斥在《百年孤独》小说开头情节里的感觉。

虽然小说推崇自然茂盛和原始动力的价值观,但在这几章里,小说显然反对权力的滥用和毫无意义的

gainst the wielding of power and meaningless hierarchies. When Aureliano Segundo marries the beautiful-but-frigid Fernanda del Carpio, the novel seems to frown upon her attempts to infuse the Buendía household with false aristocratic pretensions and hollow religious values. Throughout is a skeptical look at the institution of organized religion. The characters whom the novel celebrates—especially Aureliano Segundo and José Arcadio Buendía—are not followers of organized Catholicism. José Arcadio Buendía mocks the local priest, and Aureliano Segundo keeps both a wife and a concubine and laughs at the idea of his son becoming pope. It is certainly implied that Macondo was a better place—with more freedom, lightheartedness, and spiritual integrity—before organized religion came to the city. This is not to say that *One Hundred Years of Solitude* is an anti-religious book. On the contrary, it places great stock in miracles and in faith. But the religion in *One Hundred Years of Solitude*, like the general moral and ethic value system of the book, rests lightly on its adherents. Religion is a matter, as the earliest inhabitants of the town tell the first priest who comes to Macondo, between man and God, free of intermediaries. One Hundred Years of Solitude suggests that life is best when lived with exuberance and with few inhibitions: certainly, most of the characters in the novel seem to be uninhibited by traditional religious morals, sexual or otherwise. Thus Fernanda del Carpio is made to seem foolish for her strict adherence to Catholic principles, while Petra Cotes, Aureliano Segundo's lascivious concubine, seems to be rewarded for her promiscuous behavior with fabulous wealth.

阶级划分。当奥雷良诺·塞贡多娶了美丽但是缺乏性感的菲兰达·德卡皮奥为妻时,小说似乎对菲兰达·德卡皮奥企图把虚伪的贵族意识和空洞的宗教观念注入布恩地亚家族表示反对。同样,整部小说对正统的宗教组织也持有怀疑的态度。小说特意刻画的一些人物,特别是奥雷良诺·塞贡多及霍塞·阿卡迪奥·布恩地亚,他们都不是正统天主教的信仰者:霍塞·阿卡迪奥·布恩地亚嘲笑小镇的牧师;奥雷良诺·塞贡多既结了婚,又找情人而且对他的儿子即将成为教皇的说法耻笑不已。小说明确地暗示:在正统宗教组织到来之前,马贡多是一个更好的地方——拥有更加自由、轻松的生活空间,在精神上完美无缺。但这并不意味着《百年孤独》是一部反宗教小说。相反,小说充满了奇迹和信仰。但是小说中的信仰,诸如基本的道德和伦理观念,并不十分严格地约束信徒。在这里,宗教是一种精神本质,如同早期居民告诉来到这里的第一个牧师:在人和上帝之间不存在中介。小说主张:最理想的生活就是人们能够生活在生气勃勃、无拘无束的状态之中。诚然,小说中的大多数角色都不受传统的信仰、道德、性爱或者其他观念的约束。因而我们看到:菲兰达·德卡皮奥对天主教教义生硬死板的遵循显得愚蠢无比,而皮拉·苔列娜,奥雷良诺·塞贡多淫荡的情妇,因其滥交的行为却得到了奖赏——她获得了惊人的财富。

Chapters 12-13

Summary: Chapter 12

> *It was as if God had decided to put to the test every capacity for surprise...*
>
> (See QUOTATIONS, p.156)

The influx of modern technology that arrived in Macondo with the railroad is amazing and troubling to the citizens of the now-thriving village. But doubly confusing is the arrival in Macondo of foreign capitalists who establish a banana plantation in the village and set up their own fenced-in town right next to Macondo. Macondo rapidly becomes more cosmopolitan: the cinema, phonographs, luxury imports, and more and more prostitutes arrive in the town. It is a time of chaos and uncontrolled growth in Macondo, and Aureliano Segundo is overjoyed by the overflowing energy. The only person who remains unexcited is the ethereal Remedios the Beauty, who seems blissfully unaware of the changes going on around her. She is unaware, too, that her beauty is deadly and that men die for the sin of loving her. In fact, she remains unconcerned with love and with men throughout the novel and seems unworldly until one day she floats off the ground and up to heaven, disappearing forever.

With capitalism running rampant in Macondo, Colonel Aureliano Buendía begins to repent his decision to end the war against the Conservatives, who are facilitating the rise to pow-

第12~13章

综述：第12章

> 上帝似乎决定试验一下马贡多居民们惊愕的程度……
>
> （见第157页引文）

现在的马贡多呈现出一片繁荣的景象，居民对随着铁路开通而涌入马贡多的现代化技术感到既惊奇又困扰。但是更令居民感到大惑不解的是外国资本家的到来。外国资本家在村里开垦香蕉种植园，在马贡多的周边建造属于他们自己的市镇，并用栅栏把市镇围起来。马贡多很快变得更加现代化了：电影、留声机、奢侈的进口商品以及越来越多的妓女统统涌入小镇。对于马贡多来说，这是一个混乱的时代，小镇的发展速度达到了难以控制的地步。奥雷良诺·塞贡多拥有过剩的精力，这使得他兴奋不已。只有一个人对周围发生的一切无动于衷，这就是天真、幸福的俏姑娘蕾麦黛丝，她好像对周围所发生的一切一无所知。她甚至不知道自己的美貌是致命的，爱上她的男人们都因为亵渎纯真的罪过而纷纷死去。事实上，在整部小说中，俏姑娘蕾麦黛丝对于爱情和男人根本就漠不关心，而且她看上去似乎超凡脱俗，终于有一天，她飘离地面，飞上了天空，永远地消失了。

随着资本主义在马贡多的发展越发猖獗，加之保守党政府助长外国资本家势力的扩张，奥雷良诺·布恩地亚上校改变了他当初结束对保守党战争的决定。

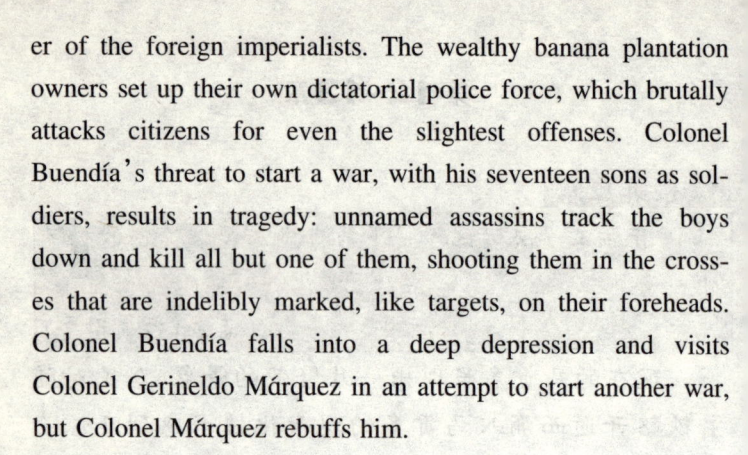

er of the foreign imperialists. The wealthy banana plantation owners set up their own dictatorial police force, which brutally attacks citizens for even the slightest offenses. Colonel Buendía's threat to start a war, with his seventeen sons as soldiers, results in tragedy: unnamed assassins track the boys down and kill all but one of them, shooting them in the crosses that are indelibly marked, like targets, on their foreheads. Colonel Buendía falls into a deep depression and visits Colonel Gerineldo Márquez in an attempt to start another war, but Colonel Márquez rebuffs him.

Summary: Chapter 13

Úrsula, meanwhile, has grown very old and notices that time is passing more quickly now than it did in the old days. She is going blind, but no one notices, because she always knows where everyone is according to his or her daily routine. Úrsula is driven by a dedication to José Arcadio II becoming pope. Nevertheless, she is deeply sad at all the tragedy that has befallen the family. When José Arcadio II goes away to seminary and Meme to school, the house becomes even emptier. Amaranta starts weaving her own shroud in preparation for death. Fernanda del Carpio gains increasing domestic control and tries again to impose her harsh, religious discipline on the household. As a result, Aureliano Segundo moves into the house of his concubine, Petra Cotes, carrying his revelry to new heights. On one occasion, he almost kills himself in an eating contest with a woman known as The Elephant. In the absence of the children, the house becomes grim and ghostly quiet. When Meme comes home from school, however, Aure-

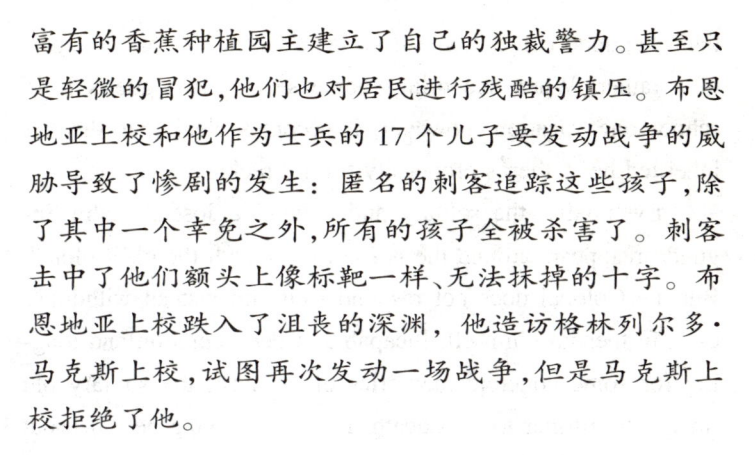

富有的香蕉种植园主建立了自己的独裁警力。甚至只是轻微的冒犯,他们也对居民进行残酷的镇压。布恩地亚上校和他作为士兵的17个儿子要发动战争的威胁导致了惨剧的发生:匿名的刺客追踪这些孩子,除了其中一个幸免之外,所有的孩子全被杀害了。刺客击中了他们额头上像标靶一样、无法抹掉的十字。布恩地亚上校跌入了沮丧的深渊,他造访格林列尔多·马克斯上校,试图再次发动一场战争,但是马克斯上校拒绝了他。

综述:第13章

这时的乌苏拉年事已高。她注意到如今时间比往常过得要快的多。她几乎快要瞎了,但是没有人发现这一点,因为她总是能根据每个人的日常活动范围判断出他们所在的位置。她为霍塞·阿卡迪奥第二能成为教皇而操劳着。然而降临家族的灾难使她深深地陷入了痛苦之中。当霍塞·阿卡迪奥第二离家前往神学院、梅梅去上学之后,家里变得更加冷清了。阿玛兰塔开始给自己缝制寿衣以便为死亡做准备。菲兰达·德卡皮奥进一步掌控了家庭的控制权,她又开始对家庭事务制定苛刻的清规戒律。结果奥雷良诺·塞贡多搬到他的情人——佩特娜·柯特家里去住了,把他的狂欢推向了一个新的高潮。他曾经在与一个叫做"大象"的女人的比吃大赛中几乎丧命。在空巢的家中,屋里变得异常的恐怖,死一般的寂静。然而当梅梅从学校返回家中时,奥雷良诺·塞贡多也从佩特娜·柯特那里

liano Segundo comes home from Petra Cotes's to play the part of a father. When she brings home seventy-two guests from school one vacation, however, it becomes clear that she has inherited her father's propensity toward reckless abandon.

Eventually, the solitary and enigmatic José Arcadio Segundo reappears around the house to talk with the old Colonel. But the Colonel does not respond well and instead withdraws even further into himself. Incapable of deep emotion and longing for some concrete memories of his past, the solitary old man drifts further toward death. He stops making new fish out of gold, which is his one constant hobby, and instead makes only a few fish before melting them down to start all over again. Finally, one morning, he passes away.

Analysis : Chapters 12-13

There is a certain amount of irony in García Márquez's proposition that modern technology and the pace of modern change confuse the villagers' sense of reality. After all, these are people who seem unfazed by the plainly miraculous. This reversal of the reader's expectation is in fact a reversal of social norms: supernatural phenomena are expected in Macondo, but technological phenomena seem unreal. The reversal is especially apparent with the arrival of the train, which brings the confusion of modernity to Macondo: "It was as if God had decided to put to the test every capacity for surprise and was keeping the inhabitants of Macondo in a permanent alteration between excitement and disappointment, doubt and revelation, to such an extreme that no one knew for certain where the limits of reality lay." As *One Hundred Years of Solitude* progresses, technology takes the place of supernatural events: the

回来扮演父亲的角色。有一次梅梅把72位客人从学校带回家中度假,这说明她继承了父亲狂放不羁的性格特征。

这时,孤独、神秘的霍塞·阿卡迪奥·塞贡多重新出现在家里,他找到老上校并与之交谈,但是上校不但没有对他做出积极反应,反而更加内敛了。因无法激发内心的情感以及恢复往日具体的记忆,这个孤独的老人沦落到了死亡的边缘。他停止了用金子制作新的小金鱼——他长久以来持续不变的嗜好。相反,他先把制作好的小金鱼溶化掉,然后用溶化后的金子重新开始制作下一批数量有限的小金鱼。最后,在一天早晨,他去世了。

品评:第12~13章

加西亚·马尔克斯创作的主题含有一定成分的戏剧性反讽:现代化技术和现代变革的节奏迷惑了村民的现实感。毕竟,平凡的奇迹好像无法扰乱这些人。读者期待的逆转事实上就是社会观念的逆转:超自然的现象可以在马贡多得到应验,但是科学技术的现象却是虚幻的。火车的到来使得这种逆转就特别的明显,它给马贡多带来了现代化的混乱:"上帝似乎决定试验一下马贡多居民们惊愕的程度,让他们经常处于高兴与失望、怀疑和承认的交替之中,以致没有一个人能够肯定地说现实的限度究竟在哪里。"随着小说情节的发展,科学技术代替了超自然事件的发生:香蕉公司的工程师们被称为:"借助了过去上帝才有的力量。"

engineers of the banana company are said to be "endowed with means that had been reserved for Divine Providence in former times."

There is also a real political and historical message behind this reversal of expectations. García Márquez is attempting to convey the extent of confusion that Western industrial technology created in the lives of Latin Americans, whose minds were comfortable with the mythic and the supernatural, but for whom an adjustment to modern culture was extremely difficult. The townspeople reject the cinema because technology here is the stuff of unreality and illusions, whereas the appearances of the ghosts of José Arcadio Buendía, or of Melquíades, are taken to be genuine phenomena. As readers of *One Hundred Years of Solitude*, we are expected to view both magic and technology as real, accepting that the difference between them is, at least in the novel, a question of perspective rather than objective fact.

The banana plantation later becomes the most tragic disturbance for the town because of the influx of new money and new inhabitants that it brings. The perfectly ordered village that José Arcadio Buendía founded becomes noisy and chaotic. Only Remedios the Beauty retains her sense of calm and her innocence. She is one of the most perplexing characters in the novel, because she seems to lack a personality of her own— she functions only as a symbol. Incapable of the deep introspec-tion characteristic of the Buendías, Remedios the Beauty lacks a sense of self and an ability to empathize with others. She is driven only by animal emotions, and her only characteristics are innocence and heartbreaking beauty. She functions, then, not as a living person within the novel, but simply

在这个预期逆转的后面还隐含着现实的政治和历史寓意。加西亚·马尔克斯试图传递这样一种混乱的程度：西方工业技术渗透了拉美人民的生活，但是适应这种现代文化对于他们来说是极为困难的，因为他们的心灵充满了神话和超自然的力量。居民反对看电影，因为他们认为电影技术是一种非现实、虚幻的东西，但是他们反倒把霍塞·阿卡迪奥·布恩地亚或者梅尔加德斯幽灵的出现看成是真实存在的现象。作为《百年孤独》的读者，我们希望把魔幻和科技都当作真实存在的东西并且接受这样一个事实：魔幻和科技之间的区别，至少在小说里，与其说它们是客观存在的事实，不如说是人们在看待问题的角度上存在着差异。

由于香蕉种植热带来了新投资并且引发了移民潮，给马贡多带来了最为严重的混乱。这个曾经由霍塞·阿卡迪奥·布恩地亚创建的、秩序井然的村庄顿时变成了一个喧闹、躁动的城镇。只有俏姑娘蕾麦黛丝处在平静当中，显得天真无邪。她是小说中最令人感到困惑不解的一个角色。她看上去缺乏自身的个性特征，在小说中仅仅起到了一个象征的作用。由于没有深刻的自省能力，这一点是布恩地亚家族所共有的性格特征，俏姑娘蕾麦黛丝缺乏自我意识而且无法体会别人的感受。她只受到动物本能的驱使，惟一的特征就是天真无邪和销人魂魄的美丽。她在小说中起到的作用不是一个活生生的人，而是一个美丽纯真的象

as a symbol of the beautiful innocence that Macondo has lost—an innocence similar to that of Adam and Eve before they ate the forbidden fruit and gained knowledge of nakedness and sin. Remedios the Beauty sees nakedness as the only natural way to walk around the house. In the tainted world of modern Macondo, corrupted by too much knowledge and technology, Remedios is a relic and a reminder of the past. It comes as a tragic real-ization that she is, in fact, too pure for the world, and she sim-ply floats skyward and disappears, presumably summoned back into the heavens.

While Remedios the Beauty's untainted innocence seems reminiscent of the Garden of Eden, Úrsula's musings on time in Chapter 13 call to mind the Old Testament as a whole. She reflects that, in the old days, children grew up more slowly and time affected people more gently. This notion is similar to the early parts of the Bible, where people live for vast numbers of years; as the Bible moves on, it depicts time passing more quickly. García Márquez has used a similar technique to determine the pacing of *One Hundred Years of Solitude*. At first, the future stretches out limitlessly—people live without fear of death, and there is more than enough room in the world for all their children. As the book moves on, however, death plays a bigger role and time begins to pass so quickly that it becomes hard to keep up with. For instance, children grow into adults in the space of a chapter or two. In addition to paralleling the Bible, this increase in the pace of time reflects the span of a human life, where time seems limitless at

征,而这恰恰是马贡多已经失去了的特质。俏姑娘蕾麦黛丝拥有的美丽和纯真类似于亚当和夏娃在偷吃禁果以及知道裸露和罪恶之前所代表的那份纯真。俏姑娘蕾麦黛丝把裸露着身体在房子周围走来走去仅仅看作是再自然不过的事情。在这个堕落的现代化世界里,马贡多被过多的知识和技术腐化了,而蕾麦黛丝是一个活化石,提醒人们回忆过去的时光。人们意识到了这样一个残酷的事实,实际上俏姑娘蕾麦黛丝简直太纯洁了,以致于她无法留在尘世,有一天她突然飘上了天空并且消失了,可能是被上帝召回了天堂。

俏姑娘蕾麦黛丝未经玷污的纯真使人们联想到了伊甸园,而乌苏拉在第 13 章对于时间的冥想不禁让人想起圣经的旧约。她回想起在过去的时候,孩子们成长的过程是比较缓慢的,时间对人的影响也是潜移默化的。这种意识类似于圣经的开头部分,在那个时候人们生活在漫长的时间里;随着圣经故事的发展,时间流逝的速度越来越快。加西亚·马尔克斯运用类似的手法来设计《百年孤独》故事情节发展的节奏。这一点首先体现在:起初,未来的发展没有尽头——在人们的生活当中根本没有死亡的概念,而对于所有的子孙后代来说,他们拥有的空间是广阔的。然而随着小说故事情节的发展,死亡的主题凸现,而且时间开始迅速流逝以致于人们似乎无法跟上它的节奏。例如,在一个或者两个章节的故事情节里,一个婴儿转眼间就长大成人了。除了效仿圣经的故事情节之外,时间节律的加快同样也反映了人类生命跨度的特征——人

first but starts to fly by as the years go on. In that sense, Macondo is like a human being, *One Hundred Years of Solitude*, its biography.

As time passes more quickly, the cycles of repetition that have been present throughout the novel happen on a smaller and smaller scale. Aureliano keeps on making gold fishes, but now he melts them down again and again and reworks them, closing himself up in that minute repetition. Blind Úrsula is able to function because she realizes that the people in the Buendía house repeat the same routines every day with no variation. And, just before Colonel Aureliano Buendía dies, he has a dream in which he realizes that he has dreamed the same dream every night for years. All these occurrences are symptoms of the spiral that winds around the Buendías, binding them in a web of the past that they cannot escape.

Chapters 14–15

Summary: Chapter 14

During the mourning period for Colonel Aureliano Buendía, Fernanda del Carpio gives birth to her third child with Aureliano Segundo, Amaranta Úrsula. For years, the elder Amaranta, who is the last living second-generation Buendía, has been retreating into her memories. Amaranta lives more in her lonely, regretful past than in the present. Visited with a premonition of her own death, she begins to

之初,时间似乎是无限的,但是随着年龄的增长,时间开始飞快流逝。从这一层意义上说,马贡多就好像一个人,而《百年孤独》就是它的一部自传。

当时间流逝的速度不断加快,这种贯穿于小说始终、循环往复式的周期越来越短。奥雷良诺不断地制作小金鱼,但是他现在一遍又一遍地把制作好的小金鱼溶化掉,然后再重新制作,把自己封闭在这些微不足道的重复当中。乌苏拉虽然失明了,但是她仍能判断出每个人所在的位置,因为她了解到家里人每天都在固定的范围内重复地活动着,没有任何的变化。就在奥雷良诺·布恩地亚上校去世之前,他做了一个梦,在梦中他意识到他多年来每天晚上都在做着一个相同的梦。这些所有发生的事情呈现了一种螺旋式发展的特征,它们在布恩地亚家族中不断地轮回着,就如同把他们束缚在了一张无法逃避过去的网上。

第 14~15 章

综述:第 14 章

在奥雷良诺·布恩地亚上校的服丧期,菲兰达·德卡皮奥和奥雷良诺·塞贡多生下了他们的第三个孩子——阿玛兰塔·乌苏拉。 多年来,老阿玛兰塔——布恩地亚家族第二代中最后一位幸存者,一直躲避在记忆当中。与其说阿玛兰塔活在现在,不如说她孤独地沉湎于对过去的悔恨之中。她预感到了死亡的来临,开始为自己缝制寿衣。当制作完成后,她向全镇人宣布她将在黄昏时刻离世并且愿意为活着的人向死

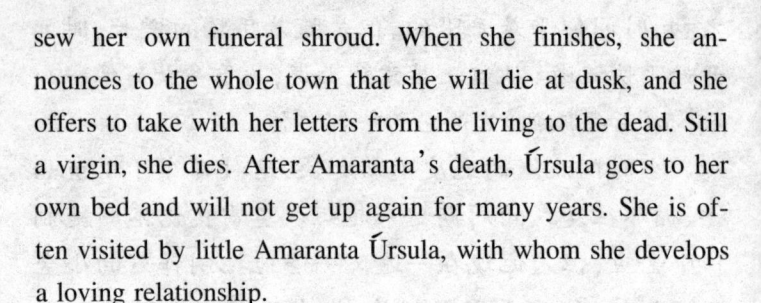

sew her own funeral shroud. When she finishes, she announces to the whole town that she will die at dusk, and she offers to take with her letters from the living to the dead. Still a virgin, she dies. After Amaranta's death, Úrsula goes to her own bed and will not get up again for many years. She is often visited by little Amaranta Úrsula, with whom she develops a loving relationship.

Meme, the first daughter of Aureliano Segundo and Fernanda del Carpio, grows up as frivolous as her father, only feigning interest in the clavichord that her mother forces her to study. With her father, Meme develops a companionship based on shared interests and mutual distaste for Fernanda. She befriends a few American girls and starts to socialize with them, even learning a little English. Meme falls madly in love with Mauricio Babilonia, a mechanic working for the banana plantation who courts her bluntly and shamelessly and whose openness and solemnity entrance Meme. He is followed always by yellow butterflies. Fernanda discovers them kissing in a movie theater and confines the lovesick Meme to the house. When she deduces that Mauricio Babilonia sneaks into the house every night to make love to Meme, she posts a guard in the backyard. When Babilonia returns once more, the guard shoots him, shattering his spine and paralyzing him for the rest of his life.

Summary: Chapter 15

The tragic paralysis of Mauricio Babilonia traumatizes Meme, striking her mute. Scandalized by Meme's behavior, Fernanda takes her on the long journey back to the city where Fernanda was born. Meme is interred in a convent, where she

去的人捎信。一直到死,她还是一个处女。乌苏拉从此以后多年来卧床不起。小阿玛兰塔经常来看望她,两人感情日渐深厚。

奥雷良诺·塞贡多和菲兰达·德卡皮奥的长女——梅梅和她父亲一样轻浮、狂放不羁。她在母亲的逼迫下佯装对古钢琴学习感兴趣。基于对菲兰达的嫌恶,父女两人同病相怜,成为了好朋友。梅梅和一些美国女孩子交上了朋友并且开始与她们交往,甚至还学了一些英语。她疯狂地恋上了毛里西奥·巴比洛尼亚,他是一名机修工,在香蕉种植园工作,他直率、大胆地追求梅梅,而且他的率真和庄重深深地吸引着梅梅。一群黄蝴蝶总是萦绕着毛里西奥·巴比洛尼亚上下纷飞。菲兰达发现他们在电影院接吻,一气之下把患相思病的梅梅监禁在屋里。当菲兰达猜到毛里西奥·巴比洛尼亚每天晚上悄悄地溜进屋里与梅梅做爱时,她在后院里安排了一个警卫。当毛里西奥·巴比洛尼亚又一次溜进院里时,警卫开枪打中了他,子弹击碎了他的脊椎骨。毛里西奥·巴比洛尼亚在瘫痪中度过了余生。

综述·第15章

毛里西奥·巴比洛尼亚悲剧性的瘫痪致使梅梅在心灵上遭受了巨大的打击,她患上了失语症。菲兰达对梅梅的行为感到耻辱,她带上梅梅长途跋涉,回到了她当年出生的那个城市。梅梅被监禁在了一个女修

spends the rest of her life thinking about Mauricio Babilonia. Months after she arrives, one of the nuns from the convent appears at the Buendía house with Meme's illegitimate child, fathered by Mauricio Babilonia, whom Fernanda keeps hidden in Colonel Aureliano Buendía's old workshop. Ashamed of Meme's actions, she pretends that the child is a foundling. He bears the name of Aureliano (II).

Meanwhile, José Arcadio Segundo, the silent and solitary brother of Aureliano Segundo, has been organizing the banana plantation workers to strike in protest of the inhumane working conditions. Macondo is placed under martial law, and the workers respond by sabotaging the plantation. The government reacts by inviting more than 3,000 of the workers to gather for a meeting with the leadership of the province and to resolve their differences. The meeting is a trick, and the army surrounds the workers with machine guns and methodically kills them all. The corpses are collected onto a train and dumped into the sea. José Arcadio Segundo, taken for dead, is thrown onto the train as well, but he manages to jump off the train and walk back to Macondo. There, he is horrified to discover that all memory of the massacre has been wiped out—none of the people of Macondo remember what happened, and they refuse to believe José Arcadio Segundo when he tells them. A heavy, unrelenting rain falls on the town and does not stop, destroying any physical traces of the massacre.

The army and the government continue exterminating any surviving union leaders and denying all reports of a massacre. Finally, José Arcadio Segundo is tracked down at the Buendía house, where he is hiding in Melquíades' old room. Looking in the room, which seems to all the Buendías exactly as it was

道院里，她在那里依靠思念毛里西奥·巴比洛尼亚打发余生。几个月之后，女修道院的一个修女出现在布恩地亚家族，带来了梅梅和毛里西奥·巴比洛尼亚的私生子。菲兰达一直把这个私生子藏匿在奥雷良诺·布恩地亚上校过去工作过的老手工作坊里。由于耻于梅梅的行为，她伪称这个孩子是一个不知父母为谁的弃婴。这个孩子被命名为奥雷良诺第二。

与此同时，沉默寡言、孤独的霍塞·阿卡迪奥·塞贡多——奥雷良诺·塞贡多的哥哥，正在组织香蕉工人罢工以抵制香蕉种植园非人的工作条件。这时马贡多被戒严了，工人们破坏了香蕉种植园作为回应。政府邀请3000多工人聚集在一起与当局领导通过谈判来解决他们的争端。然而这个谈判是一个骗局，用机关枪武装起来的军队包围了聚集的工人，有预谋地将他们全部杀害了。工人们的尸体被装上了火车并且全部被抛到大海里去了。霍塞·阿卡迪奥·塞贡多，误以为已死，也被扔上了火车，但是他设法跳下火车，沿途走回了马贡多。回来后，他吃惊地发现人们有关大屠杀的记忆全部被抹掉了——在马贡多没有任何一个人还记得发生了什么，而且当他告诉他们发生了什么事时，居民们根本就不相信他。一场无情的大雨降临了小镇，而且似乎没有停止的迹象，把大屠杀的蛛丝马迹洗刷得一干二净。

军队和政府继续根除任何一个侥幸逃脱的工会组织者而且否认所有有关屠杀的说法。最后，士兵追踪霍塞·阿卡迪奥·塞贡多来到了布恩地亚宅邸，霍塞·阿卡迪奥·塞贡多隐匿在梅尔加德斯当初住过的

in the days of Melquíades, the soldiers see only decay, as if the room has aged immeasurably. They do not notice José Arcadio Segundo. Terrified of the outside world after the massacre, José Arcadio Segundo takes refuge in the gypsy's old room, studying Melquíades' incomprehensible manuscripts. Slowly, he becomes dead to the outside world and his obsession leads him to a loss of sanity. José Arcadio Segundo lives only for the study of his texts and to preserve the memory of the 3,000 who died in the massacre.

Analysis: Chapters 14-15

In addition to signaling the Buendía family's continuing spiral toward its eventual destruction, the dual tragedies of Meme's ruined love affair and the massacre of the striking banana workers allow the later generations of Buendías to revisit the events that shaped the lives of their ancestors. After Mauricio Babilonia is shot on Fernanda del Carpio's command, Meme is forced to become a nun in the same gloomy convent, in the same grim city, where her mother Fernanda lived. It is not difficult to see in Meme's return to Fernanda's birthplace an echo of the beginning, in which the child fulfils the grim destiny from which her mother was rescued by Aureliano Segundo's love. And in José Arcadio Segundo's allegiance with the strikers, too, lies a parallel—he has taken the place of Colonel Aureliano Buendía, who, in an earlier generation, fought for the rights of the working class. Later, after the massacre, he also inherits Colonel Aureliano's disillusionment with war and solitary nature, locking himself up with Melquíades's manuscripts, like the Colonel locked himself up

老房子里。士兵在房里搜寻,这间布恩地亚家族的屋子看上去与梅尔加德斯活着的时候完全一样,眼前疮痍满目,好像说不清这个房子盖了有多少年头了。士兵们在这间屋里并没有发现霍塞·阿卡迪奥·塞贡多。在经历了大屠杀之后,霍塞·阿卡迪奥·塞贡多对外界产生了恐惧感,他躲避在吉普赛人的老房子里,潜心研究梅尔加德斯令人费解的手稿。他慢慢地变得对外界一无所知,对于手稿的沉迷导致他丧失了理智。霍塞·阿卡迪奥·塞贡多此时活在世上的目的似乎仅仅是为了研究手稿以及保存在大屠杀中有3000多工人丧生的记忆。

品评:第 14~15 章

除了预示布恩地亚家族在不断的轮回中逐渐走向毁灭之外,梅梅爱情的终结和罢工的香蕉工人被屠杀的双重悲剧致使布恩地亚家族的后代重蹈了他们祖先命运的覆辙。在毛里西奥·巴比洛尼亚被菲兰达·德卡皮奥德指使的警卫射伤之后,梅梅被迫成为了修女。她生活在她母亲菲兰达曾经住过的同一个女修道院和同一个阴森恐怖的城市。我们不难看出,梅梅回归到母亲出生的地方重复了母亲的命运。她正在重复母亲菲兰达过去凄凉的命运,而正是父亲奥雷良诺·塞贡多的爱情把母亲从这种命运中拯救了出来。霍塞·阿卡迪奥·塞贡多与罢工的香蕉工人同仇敌忾同样类似一个轮回:他似乎是上一代人奥雷良诺·布恩地亚上校的化身,为争取工人阶级的权利而战。但是在经历大屠杀之后,他像布恩地亚上校一样,对战争抱有的理想幻灭了。他还继承了布恩地亚上校孤独的

with little fishes. With her typical wisdom, Úrsula Iguarán notices the generational similarities: "It's as if the world were repeating itself," she remarks.

The contrast between the harrowing nature of the workers' massacre and the frank manner in which it is told can be explained by García Márquez's use of personal recollections in the construction of his fictional plots. There is very little sensationalist talk about blood and gore. The machine gun fire is compared to a "whirlwind," and the crowd of workers to an "onion." The episode is over in a few pages, and it is almost immediately forgotten by everyone in town except José Arcadio Segundo. But García Márquez's matter-of-fact tone does nothing to lessen the horror of the incident. On the contrary, the massacre seems all the more brutal for the machine-like quality of its perpetrators and for the concise prose in which it is told, as if the author himself was too horrified to spend much time writing about the incident. This is not surprising, since the massacre was inspired by a horrific episode in García Márquez's own experience. As a child, García Márquez lived near a banana plantation, and, when the workers at the plantation went on strike, they were killed with machine guns and thrown into the ocean.

It is not only García Márquez's experiences and memories that are folded into the narrative but his political beliefs as well. In the story of Colonel Aureliano Buendía's fight for the Liberal party, it is impossible not to notice García Márquez's sympathy for the Liberals and their cause and his disdain for

性格,把自己关进屋子,潜心研究梅尔加德斯的手稿,就像布恩地亚上校把自己关起来制作小金鱼一样。根据自己百般灵验的判断,乌苏拉观察到了每一代人的共同点,她说:"仿佛世上的一切都在循环。"

工人被屠杀的惨烈本质与其直白的叙述方法之间形成了对比,这可以从加西亚·马尔克斯运用个人记忆来建构小说情节的表现手法中获得诠释。小说几乎没有渲染血腥事件和杀戮时刻。机关枪的开火被形容为一股"旋风",聚集的工人被比喻为一个"洋葱"。这段大屠杀情节的描写只占了几页的篇幅,除了霍塞·阿卡迪奥·塞贡多外,小镇的每个人几乎在片刻之间就把大屠杀事件忘却了。但是加西亚·马尔克斯直白的叙述口吻并没有削弱大屠杀的恐怖感。相反,比起大屠杀本身,大屠杀实施者的机器般本性看上去似乎更具残忍性。同样,小说简洁的散文式描写方法也更具渲染性,作者好像感到太恐怖了以致于无法花费太多的时间来描写大屠杀事件。其实这并不奇怪,因为小说中大屠杀的创作灵感来源于作者加西亚·马尔克斯亲身经历过的一个恐怖事件。在孩提时代,加西亚·马尔克斯住在一个香蕉种植园附近,当种植园的工人进行罢工时,他们被机关枪所射杀,而且尸体被抛进了海里。

不仅加西亚·马尔克斯的个人经历和记忆融进了小说的叙事当中,而且他的政治观念也掺杂其中。在叙述奥雷良诺·布恩地亚上校为自由党而战的情节中,我们不可能不注意到加西亚·马尔克斯对自由党分子和他们反叛的原因抱有同情,而对于腐败的保守

the corrupt Conservative government. These political parties, and the war between them, are not entirely fictional. Instead, the parties and the uprisings are fictionalized incarnations of the political struggles in García Márquez's native Colombia. Similarly, it is difficult to read García Márquez's chapters about the banana company in Macondo without recognizing that the underlying subtext is the history of Western imperialism in Latin America. In *One Hundred Years of Solitude*, García Márquez depicts the capitalist imperialism of the banana companies as voracious and harmful to the inhabitants of Macondo. Capitalism and imperialism, supported by the country's Conservative government, bring corruption and brutality to Macondo and oppression to the inhabitants. García Márquez is not simply writing fiction but is telling a story about politics and life in Latin America, speaking as the representative of an entire culture. *One Hundred Years of Solitude* is fiction that shoulders the burdens of social and cultural responsibility.

Chapters 16–17

Summary: Chapter 16

The rain that begins the night of the massacre does not stop for almost five years. Imprisoned by the rain, Aureliano Segundo lapses into a restful quiet, abandoning the debauchery of his earlier years. He begins to care for the children, Amaranta Úrsula and Aureliano (II), Meme's illegitimate son, who has finally escaped from the room where Fernanda del Carpio had been hiding him. Úrsula, bed-ridden, grows more senile

党政府持以鄙视的态度。小说中的这些政党以及它们之间的战争并不完全是虚构的。相反,小说中的政党以及反抗斗争是加西亚·马尔克斯母国——哥伦比亚国内政治斗争虚构的化身。同样,我们也不难发现,加西亚·马尔克斯描写有关香蕉公司在马贡多的这些情节,毋庸置疑,其潜在的含义是暗含了一部西方资本主义在拉丁美洲的殖民史。在《百年孤独》小说中,加西亚·马尔克斯是这样来描写资本家的帝国主义行径的:对于马贡多的居民来说,香蕉公司是贪得无厌的,而且它们的到来是有害无益的。保安党政府支持的资本主义和殖民主义,给马贡多带来的是腐化与野蛮,给居民带来的是无情的镇压。加西亚·马尔克斯不仅创作了一部小说,而且还讲述了一个有关拉丁美洲政治和生活的故事,他发出的呼声代表了整个拉美文化。《百年孤独》是一部肩负着社会和文化责任重担的小说。

第 16~17 章

综述:第16章

　　大屠杀之夜开始的这场雨几乎下了五年都没有停止。雨束缚了人们的活动,奥雷良诺·塞贡多陷入了沉静之中,结束了他曾经放荡不羁的生活。他开始关注起孩子们——阿玛兰塔·乌苏拉和奥雷良诺第二的生活了。奥雷良诺第二是梅梅的私生子,他最终从菲兰达·德卡皮奥藏匿他的房子逃了出来。卧床不起的

and less coherent, becoming merely a plaything for the children, who learn from her the stories of their ancestors. The rain eats away at the house and reduces Aureliano Segundo's vast fortune to nothing, as all the animals he bred with Petra Cotes die in the flooding. Fernanda occupies herself with contacting the telepathic doctors, who are trying to heal her from a disease of the uterus, and she also occupies herself by tormenting her husband, Aureliano Segundo, who loses his temper and breaks every valuable thing in the house. Aureliano Segundo, in turn, occupies himself with an attempt to find the fortune in gold coins that Úrsula has hidden somewhere in the backyard of the house. When the rains finally end, Macondo has suffered a precipitous decline. The banana plantations have been washed away, and the town is receding backward into memory.

Summary: Chapter 17

With the end of the rains, Úrsula gets out of bed and tries to rehabilitate the Buendía house. She discovers José Arcadio Segundo, who has been sequestered in his room for years, trying to decipher the ancient prophecies of the gypsy Melquíades. Returning to the house of his concubine Petra Cotes and finding all their animals dead, they are forced to struggle as never before to make ends meet. Their parties are merely humble replicas of their old festivals of debauchery, but they are as happy as they have ever been, once again falling madly in love with each other. Aureliano Segundo finds himself spending less and less time with the children, who are swiftly aging. Aureliano (II) falls into the pattern of the family's tall, thin, solitary Aurelianos. Úrsula continues to

乌苏拉越来越衰弱和糊涂了,对于孩子们来说,她仅仅是一个老玩偶而已。孩子们从她那里听说了一些有关祖先们的故事。大雨侵蚀了房屋,把奥雷良诺·塞贡多的巨大财产冲洗一空,因为他和佩特娜·柯特饲养的牲畜全被洪水淹死了。菲兰达整天忙于与一个心灵感应的医生取得联系。这个未曾谋面的医生正试图治疗她的子宫疾病。同时,她不断地折磨她的丈夫——奥雷良诺·塞贡多,以致奥雷良诺·塞贡多大发雷霆,把屋里所有值钱的东西全都砸碎了。奥雷良诺·塞贡多此时却忙着探寻乌苏拉藏在房屋后院某处的金币。当雨最终停下来的时候,马贡多遭受了惨不忍睹的衰败。香蕉种植园被雨水冲走了,整个小镇退缩到人们的脑海当中,成为了永远的记忆。

综述:第17章

伴随着大雨的停止,乌苏拉从病榻上下来了,她想修缮布恩地亚家族的老宅。她发现霍塞·阿卡迪奥·塞贡多多年来一直隐居在他的住处,潜心破译吉普赛人梅尔加德斯遗留下来的古老预言。奥雷良诺·塞贡多又回到情妇佩特娜·柯特身边,他发现他们饲养的牲畜都死了。为了应对入不敷出的生活,他们被迫以前所未有的精力艰苦奋斗。但是他们又恢复了往日的快乐和幸福,两人再一次疯狂地坠入了爱河。奥雷良诺·塞贡多发现自己与孩子们呆在一起的时间越来越少了,孩子们成长的速度飞快。奥雷良诺第二继承了家族中奥雷良诺一族高大、瘦弱的身体特征以及孤独的性格。乌苏拉日渐衰老,旧病复发,她活了将近120

regress into her past, eventually dying at more than 120 years old. Rebeca, José Arcadio's widow, also dies during this time.

A hellish heat wave descends on the town, and the townspeople begin to believe that they are plagued. Birds die in droves, and a strange, semi-human creature, the Wandering Jew, is discovered in the streets. The town assumes a broken-down, abandoned feel, and it fills up with nostalgia of its former prosperity. In the midst of this poverty, Aureliano Segundo devotes himself to raising the money to send Amaranta Ursula to Europe for her education, but his great strength of former years has left him, and he is dying. José Arcadio Segundo, too, is living his last days, and he is finally making progress in deciphering Melquíades' prophecies and in initiating Aureliano (II) into both the pursuit of prophetic knowledge and the history of Macondo. Finally, Aureliano Segundo is able to send Amaranta Úrsula to Brussels. His task complete, he dies at the same instant as his twin brother José Arcadio Segundo, whose last words are a reminder to Aureliano (II) about the almost-forgotten massacre of the striking workers. In the confusion of the burial, Aureliano Segundo and José Arcadio Segundo's coffins are mixed up, and each is buried in the other's grave.

Analysis: Chapters 16-17

The nearly five-year flood that deluges Macondo, practically erasing all trace of the banana company from the land, parallels the Biblical flood that covered the earth in the time of Noah. Then, as in *One Hundred Years of Solitude*, the world had become full of wicked people, and in the Bible the

多岁才慢慢地死去。霍塞·阿卡迪奥的寡妇——蕾贝卡也在这一时期去世了。

一股地狱般的热浪袭击了马贡多,居民们开始相信瘟疫降临了。鸟类成群结队地死去,人们在大街上发现了一个怪模怪样的、半人半兽的怪物——一个流浪的犹太人。小镇看上去已经破败不堪,弥漫着荒凉的气息,使人对往日繁荣的景象充满了怀旧之情。在贫寒交加之际,奥雷良诺·塞贡多为了送阿玛兰塔·乌苏拉去欧洲求学,竭尽全力筹措资金,但是他丧失了年轻时旺盛的精力,已濒临死亡的边缘。与此同时,霍塞·阿卡迪奥·塞贡多也处在生命的最后日子里,他最终在破译梅尔加德斯的预言研究方面取得了进展,并且引导奥雷良诺第二开始探究古老手稿的预言以及马贡多的历史。奥雷良诺·塞贡多最终实现了送阿玛兰塔·乌苏拉去布鲁塞尔求学的愿望。夙愿得偿之后,奥雷良诺·塞贡多和他的双胞胎哥哥霍塞·阿卡迪奥·塞贡多在同一时刻去世了。霍塞·阿卡迪奥·塞贡多临终前给奥雷良诺第二留下的遗言是那个几乎被人们忘却的罢工工人被屠杀的事件。在埋葬他们时发生了混乱,奥雷良诺·塞贡多和霍塞·阿卡迪奥·塞贡多的棺材被搞混了,两个人被分别葬在了对方的墓穴里。

品评:第16~17章

将近下了五年的大雨引发的洪水淹没了马贡多,把香蕉公司存在的痕迹从土地上冲刷得几乎一干二净。这一点类似于圣经的典故:在诺亚时期,洪水淹没了整个大地。如同《百年孤独》小说中的世界一样,世

cleansing flood obliterates them. And it is possible to read the years of rain in *One Hundred Years of Solitude* as ordained by God, in mourning for the massacred workers, and as a cleansing agent in Macondo. Another, more insidious possibility presents itself, however. We have already been told that the banana company has the capacity to bring rain, supplanting the Divine prowess of God Himself, and it is certainly implied that the replacement of God by modern technology is symptomatic of the shattered reality of Macondo. The novel hints that Mr. Brown of the banana company, the man who has replaced both God and the angel of death, has brought the rains in order to wash away all traces of the massacre and to erase memory.

With the death of José Arcadio Segundo at the end of this section, Aureliano (II) becomes the town's preserver of memories. As Aureliano (II) explores the town in the final pages of the book, he discovers that practically all its history has been forgotten: "the voracity of oblivion," García Márquez writes, "was undermining memories in a pitiless way." Úrsula Iguarán, who in her senility and extreme old age has become childlike, serves as a metaphor for the town. Shrunken in its old age and ignorant of its past, Macondo has returned almost to its infancy. As in the beginning of the town's history, gypsies come to town, and they bring the same technologies—magnets and magnifying glasses—that Melquíades once brought. "The town [is] so defeated and its inhabitants so removed from the rest of the world" that the gypsy gimmicks are once again the source of wonderment for the few inhabitants left in town. Úrsula's statement that "time was not passing...it was turning in a circle" is more and more accurate. Macondo, like the Buendía family, seems to be stuck in a series

界里充满了邪恶的人类,在圣经故事里,洪水净化了他们。我们可以看出,在《百年孤独》小说中,多年大雨的降临是上帝的旨意,下雨是为了哀悼被屠杀的工人,在马贡多,雨水起到了清洁剂的作用。另外,还有一个隐含的可能性若隐若现。我们知道,香蕉公司拥有降雨的能力,从这一点来说,香蕉公司替代了只有上帝才能够拥有的神圣威力。这显然在暗示替代上帝权威的现代化技术是马贡多走向衰败的征兆。小说暗指这场大雨是橡胶公司的布朗先生带来的,目的是为了洗刷大屠杀的痕迹以及清除人们的记忆。布朗先生在这里显然替代了上帝的角色,同时他又是死神的化身。

在这一章节的结尾部分,随着霍塞·阿卡迪奥·塞贡多的去世,奥雷良诺第二成为了小镇记忆的惟一保存者。当奥雷良诺第二在小说结尾的最后几页里探究小镇的历史时,他发现实际上小镇的全部历史都被遗忘了,加西亚·马尔克斯在小说中写道:"贪婪的遗忘无情地吞噬着记忆。"乌苏拉·伊瓜兰在她的耄耋之年返老还童隐喻了马贡多小镇。马贡多像一个老人一样,随着年龄的增长,身体萎缩了并且遗忘了过去,好像又返回了童年时代。同马贡多小镇的早期历史一样,吉普赛人又来到小镇,他们带来了诸如磁铁和放大镜的技术——与梅尔加德斯当年带来的一模一样。"小镇是如此地折服以及居民们是如此地与世隔绝"以致于吉普赛人新奇的技术再次成为幸存的少数小镇居民们猎奇的源泉。乌苏拉的判断越来越准确了,她说:"时间停止不前了……它在原地打转。"马贡多

of circular repetitions, but it is also true that the town, and the family, are moving ever closer to their final end.

As Aureliano (II) begins to tell the story of what really happened to the banana workers, it is clear that his version of the story is quite different from the established one: "one would have thought that he was telling a hallucinated version, because it was radically opposed to the false one that historians had created and consecrated in their schoolbooks." Fictional history is seen as truth, while truth is seen as hallucination. This reversal mirrors the way in which García Márquez continues to shift the boundaries between reality and fantasy. In *One Hundred Years of Solitude*, accepted truth is sometimes less real than fantasy, and vice versa.

Chapters 18–20

Summary: Chapter 18

Aureliano (II) remains in Melquíades's old laboratory, visited occasionally by the ghost of the gypsy himself, who gives him clues and eventually helps him decipher the prophecies. Aureliano learns that the prophecies are written in Sanskrit and that they will be deciphered when they are one hundred years old. The Buendías have become poor, but they are supported by food sent to them by Aureliano Segundo's old concubine, Petra Cotes. Santa Sofía de la Piedad, the almost-invisible widow of Arcadio, finally gives up on the family, and, after a half-century of patiently tending to them, she simply walks away without any real indication of where she is going. Not long afterward, Fernanda del Carpio, who now does nothing but bemoan her fate and write to her children in

就像布恩地亚家族一样，似乎在循环往复的轮回中被卡住了，寸步难行。然而，毋庸置疑的是，马贡多小镇和布恩地亚家族同时都在不停地走向毁灭。

当奥雷良诺第二开始讲述实际发生在香蕉工人身上的故事时，显然他的故事版本与原先存在的版本之间有着很大的区别："有人可能会认为他在讲述一个虚构的版本，因为他的版本在根本上有悖于历史学家在教科书上捏造和颂扬的伪版本。"我们不但可以把虚构的历史视作真实，而且可以把真实视作虚构。这种逆转折射了加西亚·马尔克斯在现实与魔幻的领域里反复颠倒的创作技巧。在《百年孤独》小说里，接受现实有时比接受虚幻还要困难，反之亦然。

第18~20章

综述：第18章

奥雷良诺第二始终呆在梅尔加德斯的老试验室里，这个吉普赛人的幽魂偶尔前来探访他，给他提供一些线索并且帮助他逐渐破解预言。奥雷良诺第二发现这个预言是用梵语写成的，只有等到一百年以后这个预言才能被破解。布恩地亚家族已经穷困潦倒了，他们依靠奥雷良诺·塞贡多的老情人——佩特娜·柯特送来的食物勉强度日。阿卡迪奥的寡妇——桑塔·索非亚·德拉佩德，这个几乎隐形了的人，最终放弃了这个家庭。半个多世纪以来，她一直精心地照顾着这个家庭。她就这样简单地离开了，甚至没有提到她将会到哪里去。此后不久，菲兰达·德卡皮奥除了哀叹她

Europe, dies, overcome with nostalgia.

A few months after Fernanda's death, her son José Arcadio (II) returns to Macondo. He has become a solitary, dissolute man. It turns out that he has not been studying in a seminary but has, rather, been counting on inheriting a large fortune. He is trapped in the old, dilapidated house, left with nothing but his memories and his delusions of grandeur. When he discovers the gold that Úrsula Iguarán hid under her bed, he falls into debauchery, sharing with the adolescent children of the town in long nights of revelry. In his loneliness, he begins to become friendly with the solitary Aureliano (II), who is making progress in his pursuit of knowledge. The two Buendías receive a visit from the last remaining son of Colonel Aureliano Buendía, who, like his sixteen brothers before him, is shot down by the police as he stands in front of the Buendía house. The developing relationship between Aureliano (II) and José Arcadio (II) is abruptly cut off when four of the children, with whom José Arcadio (II) once celebrated at a party, kill him in his bath and steal his gold.

Summary: Chapter 19

Amaranta Úrsula returns to Macondo from Europe, bringing Gaston, her husband. He has followed her back to Macondo, even though he realizes that her love for her hometown is a nostalgic dream—energetic and determined, she wants to revitalize the house and the town, but Macondo's decline is irreversible. As Aureliano (II) wanders the rundown town, he discovers that almost no one remembers the

的命运和给远在欧洲的孩子们写信外,无所事事。她最终被怀旧之情所击垮,离开了人世。

在菲兰达死后的几个月之后,她的儿子霍塞·阿卡迪奥第二返回了马贡多。他俨然变成了一个孤独、堕落的纨绔子弟。他显然并没在神学院里完成学业,相反,指望能够继承一大笔遗产。他被困于这个陈旧、腐朽的老宅,一无所获,伴随他的只有记忆和远大的梦想。在发现了乌苏拉藏在床铺低下的金子之后,他便陷入了放荡不羁的生活,和镇上的一群青年孩子通宵达旦地寻欢作乐。当他寂寞的时候,他便和孤独的奥雷良诺第二交上了朋友。此时奥雷良诺第二正在知识的探索中艰难跋涉。这两个布恩地亚家族的成员接待一个人来访,来访者是奥雷良诺·布恩地亚上校最后一个存活下来的儿子,像他以前的16个兄弟一样,当他站在布恩地亚家族门前的时候,被警察开枪射杀了。奥雷良诺第二和霍塞·阿卡迪奥第二正在发展的友谊突然中断了,曾经和霍塞·阿卡迪奥第二一起狂欢的四个小青年在他洗澡的时候将他杀害并且偷走了他的金子。

综述:第19章

阿玛兰塔·乌苏拉同丈夫加斯东从欧洲返回了故乡马贡多。尽管加斯东意识到阿玛兰塔·乌苏拉对故乡的眷恋只是一个怀旧的梦想而已,但是他还是跟随她来到马贡多。阿玛兰塔·乌苏拉精力充沛,决心已定,她想重新振兴家族和小镇,但是马贡多的衰败已经到了无法挽回的地步。当奥雷良诺第二在破

Buendías, once the most notable family in the village. Following the family propensity toward incestuous love, Aureliano (I-I) falls in love with Amaranta Úrsula. He finds partial solace for his unrequit-ed love in his newfound friendship with a wise Catalonian bookseller, and with four young scholars he meets in the bookstore. Together, the scholars prowl the underbelly of Ma-condo, visiting whorehouses and bars. In one brothel, Aure-liano (II) is comforted by the ancient Pilar Ternera, his forgot-ten great-great-grandmother, who offers him her reliable wis-dom and intuition. He also takes a lover, a black prostitute named Nigromanta. Gaston, bored in Macondo, becomes pre-occupied with his dream of establishing an airmail service in Latin America. While Gaston is preoccupied, Aureliano (II) takes the opportunity to admit his love for Amaranta Ursula. Eventually she yields, and they become lovers.

Summary: Chapter 20

> [Aureliano] *saw the epigraph of the parchments perfectly paced ...in such a way that they coexisted in one instant.*
>
> (See QUOTATIONS, p.158)

Gaston travels to Belgium to follow up on his business plans, and, when he learns of his wife's affair, he does not return. First, the Catalonian and then Aureliano (II)'s four schol-ar friends leave Macondo, a town now locked in its quiet death throes. In the midst of the solitude of Macondo, the love affair between Aureliano (II) and Amaranta Úrsula

败不堪的小镇上游荡时,他发现镇上几乎没有一个人还记得这个曾经在村里显赫一时的布恩地亚家族了。奥雷良诺第二继承了家族乱伦的习性,他爱上了阿玛兰塔·乌苏拉。他与一个博学的加泰罗尼亚书商以及他在书店偶遇的四个青年学者建立了新的友谊,为他未得回报的爱情找到了部分安慰。这些学者们在马贡多的腹地集体游荡,光顾妓院和酒吧。在一个妓院里,奥雷良诺第二从几乎被人们遗忘的高曾祖母——快成为古董的皮拉·苔列娜那里获得了慰籍。皮拉·苔列娜给他提供了一些可靠的常识和直觉方面的知识。他也找了一个情人——一个叫做尼格罗曼塔的黑皮肤妓女。加斯东厌烦了马贡多的生活,他开始全神贯注地实现在拉丁美洲开办航空邮政的梦想。当加斯东专注于实现梦想的时候,奥雷良诺第二趁机向阿玛兰塔·乌苏拉表白了他对她的爱慕之情。阿玛兰塔·乌苏拉逐渐地屈服了,他们成为了恋人。

综述:第20章

[奥雷良诺第二]看到羊皮纸手稿上的铭文与家族成员命运发展的时空顺序完全相吻合……让它们同时存在于一瞬间。　　　　　　　　　　(见第159页引文)

　　加斯东前往比利时继续执行他的商业计划。当他获悉了妻子的风流韵事后,他再也没有回来。先是加泰罗尼亚人,紧接着奥雷良诺第二的四个学者朋友也相继离开了马贡多,此时的马贡多处于毁灭前的风雨飘摇之中。在马贡多小镇孤独的氛围中,奥雷良诺第二和阿玛兰塔·乌苏拉的爱情在炽热和幸福中延续

continues, fiercely and happily. The Buendía house falls into total disrepair, destroyed by the couple's rampant lovemaking and by the red ants that swarm everywhere. In fulfillment of the family matriarch Úrsula Iguarán's old fears about the dangers of incest, the lovers' baby, whom they also name Aureliano (III), is born with the tail of a pig. Amaranta Úrsula bleeds uncon-trollably after giving birth and soon dies. Aureliano (II) seeks comfort in the arms of Nigromanta and in drink, but he forgets about the newborn baby. When he finds the corpse, ants are feeding on it. He realizes that the line of the Buendías has come to an end. He boards himself up in the house and is finally able to decipher Melquíades' ancient prophecies. They are a description of the entire history of the Buendía family, from the time of the founding of Macondo. As he reads, he finds that the text is at that very moment mirroring his own life, describing his act of reading as he reads. And around him, an apocalyptic wind swirls, ripping the town from its founda-tions, erasing it from memory.

> *[Aureliano] had already understood that he would never leave...races condemned to one hundred years of solitude did not have a second opportunity on earth.*
>
> (See QUOTATIONS, p.160)

Analysis: Chapters 18-20

Suitably, the Buendía family spirals to its final demise with an act of incest: Aureliano (II) and Amaranta Úrsula, aunt and nephew, have a child, whom they predictably name Aureliano. They are the last two surviving members of the Buendía clan, and, like typical Buendías, they have clung to each other in solitude, isolated from the outside world. They are practical-

着。布恩地亚家族的宅邸彻底地落到了年久失修的地步，并被这对情侣的疯狂做爱以及到处成群的红蚂蚁彻底摧毁了。这对恋人重蹈了乱伦的覆辙，这是高祖母乌苏拉·伊瓜兰当年早就担忧过的事情。他们生了一个带着猪尾巴的婴儿，并给孩子取名为奥雷良诺第三。阿玛兰塔·乌苏拉分娩后血崩不止并且很快就死去了。奥雷良诺第二躺在尼格罗曼塔的臂弯里寻找安慰并且借酒浇愁，却忘记了刚刚出生的婴儿。当他发现婴儿的尸体时，一群蚂蚁正在上面吞噬着。此时他意识到布恩地亚家族的最后一代人已经灭绝了。他把自己关在房里与世隔绝起来，最终破解了梅尔加德斯的古老预言。这个预言讲述了布恩地亚家族从创建马贡多以来的整部历史。正当他解读的时候，他发现预言中的文本此刻间不仅正在折射他自己的生活，而且也描述了他目前就正在阅读预言的行为。在他的周围，一股启示性的飓风开始旋动，把小镇从地面上一扫而光，从人们的记忆中抹掉了。

[奥雷良诺第二]明白了自己已经不能跨出房间一步了……遭受百年孤独的家族，注定不会在大地上第二次出现了。

（见第161页引文）

品评：第18~20章

　　显然命运在作祟，布恩地亚家族最终以乱伦作为它走向毁灭的终点：奥雷良诺第二和阿玛兰塔·乌苏拉，姨妈和侄子的关系，生下了一个婴儿。他们预先给孩子取名为奥雷良诺。他们两人是布恩地亚家族最后存活下来的家族成员，就像典型的布恩地亚家族成员一样，他们在孤独、与世隔绝的境遇中相依为命。他们

ly the last people remaining in Macondo, a town whose history has run its course and one that is destroyed in the final lines of the book by the wind of the apocalypse. One might get the sense that it is not only Macondo but the entire world that has been destroyed in that final Apocalyptic fury, and one would not be entirely wrong. In this novel, Macondo has become a world closed in upon itself: self-referential and encompassing the full scope of human emotion and human experience. Time has run out for the Buendía family, which, in some sense, has come to represent all of humanity, with the Adam and Eve figures of José Arcadio Buendía and Ursula Iguarán as its source. The suggestion is that humans, too, will have time run out on them when their endless cycles of repeating generations finally draw to a close. "[The] history of the family," García Márquez writes, "was a...turning wheel that would have gone on spinning into eternity were it not for the progressive and irremediable wearing of the axle."

Just as the incestuous relationship between Amaranta Úrsula and Aureliano (II) signals the inward collapse of the Buendía family tree, the reading of the prophecies signals time folding up on itself. As Aureliano (II) reads, past, present, and future all happen at once. In a sense, this has been happening throughout the book: ghosts from the past have appeared and disappeared, Pilar Ternera could read the future as well as the past, and the simultaneity through which the Buendías move has made the past, the present, and the future all identical. Aureliano (II)'s final moments are like a miniature version of what's been happening all along. Time, in *One Hundred Years of Solitude*, is not a single linear progression of unique events; instead, it is an infinite number of progressions happening si-

实际上是马贡多现存的最后两个人。就像小说结尾所描写的那样，马贡多按照它既定的历史轨迹发展着，直到被一阵启示的飓风摧毁。读者也许会感觉到：不仅马贡多，而且连整个世界都被最后那场带有启示性的飓风摧毁了，这样看也并不为过。在这部小说中，马贡多是一个自我封闭的世界：它不仅自我指认而且还包含了人类所有的情感和经验。对于布恩地亚家族来说，时间似乎耗费殆尽了。在某种程度上说，布恩地亚家族是人类社会的缩影。作为布恩地亚家族的始祖，霍塞·阿卡迪奥·布恩地亚和乌苏拉·伊瓜兰是亚当和夏娃的化身。我们获得的启示是：当人类在不断繁衍的轮回中渐近结束之时，时间也随之耗费殆尽。加西亚·马尔克斯写道："家族的历史……像一个转动的车轮，它将永不停止地转动下去，直至永远。它不仅仅是为了前进而转动，而且轮轴的磨损是不能挽回的。"

如果说阿玛兰塔·乌苏拉和奥雷良诺第二的乱伦关系预示了布恩地亚家族内部的瓦解，奥雷良诺第二对于预言的解读则预示了家族崩溃时刻的到来。当奥雷良诺第二破解预言之时，过去、现在和未来的事件在一瞬之间同时发生了。从某种意义上说，这种情况的发生贯穿于整部小说：来自过去的鬼魂时而显灵时而消失；皮拉·苔列娜既可以预测未来，又可以推测过去；布恩地亚家族同时发生的事件使得过去、现在和未来处在了同一瞬间。奥雷良诺第二解读预言的最后时刻就像一面镜子，它折射了曾经发生过的所有事件。在《百年孤独》小说中，时间并不是单独事件以单线的方式在发展；相反，而是无数个事件在同一时刻同时发展，因

multaneously, in which no event can be considered unique because of its ties to both the past and the future, occurring at the same time somewhere else.

Melquíades' prophecies also occupy a peculiar place in time, since, although they are written as predictions for what will happen in the future, they are read by Aureliano (II) as an accurate history of the Buendía family. As the wind swirls around him, Aureliano (II) is finally able to decipher Melquíades' prophecies, and he finds that Melquíades has left behind a prophecy of the history of the town, which is accurate to the last detail. The text of the prophecy mirrors the reality of the town's history, so that Aureliano (II) is reading about his destruction as he experiences it. The sense of unavoidable destiny is strong: the Buendías, we realize, have long been living lives foretold-and thus, in a sense, ordained-by the all-knowing book. It might even be argued that the text of the prophecy, in fact, is identical to the book *One Hundred Years of Solitude,* and that Melquíades has served all along as a surrogate for the author, Gabriel García Márquez. Certainly the prophecy has succeeded as literature that simultaneously shapes and mirrors reality, just as *One Hundred Years of Solitude* tries to shape a fictional world while simultaneously mirroring the reality of García Márquez's Colombia. Melquíades's vision, early in the novel, of a city with walls of glass, has come true in a sense: Macondo is a city made of glass and of mirrors that reflect back the reality of the author's world.

此没有任何事件可以被认为是一个孤立存在的事件，原因是这个事件既牵扯到了过去又涉及到了未来，它们会在不同的地方在同一时刻同时发生。

　　梅尔加德斯的预言在时间其中也起到了特殊的作用。尽管手稿上的预言预示了将来才会发生的事情，但是雷良诺第二解读预言时发现它就是一部准确的布恩地亚家族发展史。当飓风在他周围开始旋动之际，雷良诺第二最终破解了梅尔加德斯的预言。他发现梅尔加德斯遗留下来的手稿是一部有关马贡多历史发展的预言，而且精确到每一个细节。手稿的预言影射了马贡多的历史，因此奥雷良诺第二在阅读预言的同时也就相当于他正在阅读自己的灭亡。小说中的宿命观使我们意识到布恩地亚家族按照预言预示的方式发展，也就是说，布恩地亚家族的命运早已被全知全能的预言所支配。值得我们讨论的是：预言实际上相当于《百年孤独》小说本身，梅尔加德斯是作者加西亚·马尔克斯的替身。事实上，预言继承了文学的特点——即塑造和折射现实，就像《百年孤独》小说一样，它既塑造了一个虚拟的世界，同时又折射了加西亚·马尔克斯的祖国——哥伦比亚的现实。在小说的开始部分，梅尔加德斯眼中有一座由玻璃墙砌成的城市，而这个玻璃城市在某种意义上说已经变成了现实：马贡多是一座由玻璃和镜子建造而成的城市，它折射了作者内心世界中的现实。

IMPORTANT QUOTATIONS EXPLAINED

> 1. *At that time Macondo was a village of twenty adobe houses, built on the bank of a river of clear water that ran a-long a bed of polished stones, which were white and enormous, like prehistoric eggs. The world was so recent that many things lacked names, and in order to indicate them it was necessary to point.*

These lines come from the very first page of the novel. They establish Macondo as a kind of Eden, recalling the biblical tale of Adam naming the animals. This parallel to the Old Testament is present throughout the book, as Macondo slowly loses its innocence by seeking too much knowledge. At the same time, however, the reference to prehistoric eggs refers to an entirely different account of the origin of the world: evolution. By beginning the book with references to two entirely different accounts of creation, García Márquez tries to tell us that, in this book, he will invent his own mythology. It will not be based solely on the Bible, nor will it be totally grounded in science. Instead, it will ask us to accept several different myths at the same time.

> 2. *Aureliano José had been destined to find with [Carmelita Montiel] the happiness that Amaranta had denied him, to have seven children, and to die in her arms of old age, but the bullet that entered his back and shattered his chest had been directed by a wrong interpretation of the cards.*

语出·有因

> 1. 当时,马贡多是个20户人家的村庄,一座座土房都盖在河岸上;河水清澈,沿着遍布石头的河床流去,河里的石头光滑、洁白,活像史前的巨蛋。这块天地还是新开辟的,许多东西都叫不出名字,为了识别它们,不得不用手来指点。

这几句话引自小说的开头。他们依照伊甸园模样建造马贡多,这不禁使人想起圣经故事中亚当给动物命名的情景。这种与旧约相比拟的手法在小说中比比皆是,又如由于渴望获取更多的知识,马贡多逐渐丧失了它的纯真。但是与此同时,这里提到的史前巨蛋则向我们提及了另外一个完全不同的世界起源,那就是进化。加西亚·马尔克斯之所以在小说一开始就向我们提及了两种截然不同的创世纪,就是因为他想告诉我们他将要创造自己的神话。这个神话既不会完全照搬圣经,也不会完全建立在科学的基础之上。相反,他要求我们在同一时刻接受几种不同的神话。

> 2. 从纸牌的占卜来看,奥雷良诺·霍塞注定要(跟卡梅丽达·蒙蒂埃尔)得到幸福——阿玛兰塔曾经拒绝给他的幸福,他们会有7个孩子,他年老以后将会死在她的怀里,可是贯穿他的脊背到胸膛的一颗子弹,显然不太理解纸牌的预示。

155

ONE HUNDRED YEARS OF SOLITUDE

Throughout *One Hundred Years of Solitude*, the idea of a predetermined fate is accepted as natural. Because time is cyclical, after all, seeing into the future can be as easy as remembering the past. In this passage from Chapter 8, however, a prediction not only foretells the future, but also actually affects it. The act of reading and interpreting has a magically powerful status in this novel. This power will be seen again in the last few pages of the book, where Aureliano (II)'s reading of the prophecies brings about the destruction of Macondo. In addition to assigning magical power to the fictional act of reading within the story, García Márquez also indicates his awareness of the importance of interpretation in any reading.

> 3. *It was as if God had decided to put to the test every capacity for surprise and was keeping the inhabitants of Macondo in a permanent alternation between excitement and disappointment, doubt and revelation, to such an extreme that no one knew for certain where the limits of reality lay. It was an intricate stew of truths and mirages that convulsed the ghost of José Arcadio Buendía with impatience and made him wander all through the house even in broad daylight.*

This quote occurs just after the arrival of the railroad, when dozens of new inventions—the phonograph, the telephone, the electric lightbulb—have flooded Macondo. The citizens of Macondo, who have accepted flying carpets and miraculous rains of yellow flowers as part of the natural way of things, doubt the reality of technological inventions. This passage therefore represents a turning point for Macondo. Whereas the citizens of Macondo once believed in the magical

贯穿于整部《百年孤独》小说之中的宿命论是被自然接受的事实。因为时间在轮回的模式中发展,预见未来与回忆过去一样简单。然而摘自第8章的这段预言不仅预示了未来,而且实际上还在影响未来的发生。具有巨大魔力的阅读和破译行为在小说中起到了重要的作用。这种魔力将在小说结尾部分的最后几页里再次得以体现,雷良诺第二解读预言的行为带来了马贡多的毁灭。除了在小说中给虚构的阅读行为赋予魔力之外,加西亚·马尔克斯同样还向我们阐明了他的观点:诠释在任何阅读中都将会起到的重要作用。

3. 上帝似乎决定要试验一下马贡多居民们惊愕的程度,让他们经常处于高兴与失望、怀疑和承认的交替之中,以致没有一个人能够肯定地说出现实的限度究竟在哪里。这是现实和幻想的混合,犹如霍塞·阿卡迪奥·布恩地亚不安的幽灵甚至大白天也在房子里踱来踱去。

铁路开通之后,琳琅满目的新发明——留声机、电话以及电灯泡等——充斥了马贡多小镇。这段引文就是引自这时。马贡多的居民可以把飞毯和奇迹般的黄花雨视为自然,他们却怀疑现代化技术发明的真实性。这段引文代表了马贡多的转折点。尽管马贡多的居民曾经只把魔幻以及神话世界当作是现实中的事情,但是他们现在却不得不同时接受科学和幻想。加西亚·马尔克斯在这里运用了幽默的技巧。霍塞·阿夫

ONE HUNDRED YEARS OF SOLITUDE

and mythi-cal world as their only reality, they must now accept both sci-ence and magic. García Márquez makes use of humor here, since one of the people who cannot believe in the telephone is the ghost of José Arcadio Buendía, who is, himelf, much more unbeliev able to modern eyes than any technological in-vention. But, in reading *One Hundred Years of Solitude*, we are asked to abandon those modern eyes in favor of the per-spective of those in Macondo. We must read at all times with an awareness of both points of view.

> 4. [Aureliano (II)] saw the epigraph of the parchments perfectly paced in the order of man's time and space: The first of the line is tied to a tree and the last is being eaten by the ants...Melquíades had not put events in the order of a man's conventional time, but had concentrated a century of daily episodes in such a way that they coexisted in one instant.

In the final pages of *One Hundred Years of Solitude*, Aureliano (II) deciphers the parchments and discovers that they collapse time so that the entire history of Macondo occurs in a single instant. Although García Márquez has written the novel in a mostly chronological fashion, there have been hints of this overlapping of time throughout the book: ghosts from the past appear in the present; the future takes its shape based on the actions of the past; amnesia plunges the citizens of Macondo into a perpetual present with neither past nor future. In other words, time in Macondo has always unfolded strangely. Only in this final moment do we find out that in Macondo, there are two kinds of time: linear and cyclical. Both have al-

迪奥·布恩·地亚的幽灵无法理解技术比如电话,而他自己对于现代的眼光而言却比任何科技发明更难以让人理解。但是在阅读《百年孤独》小说的时候,作者要求我们放弃使用现代的眼光来审视小说的方式,而采用马贡多居民的视角来审视小说。有时,我们必须有意识地结合上述两种视角来阅读小说。

4. [奥雷良诺第二]看到羊皮纸手稿上的铭文与家族成员命运发展的时空顺序完全吻合:家族中的第一个人将被绑在树上,家族中的最后一个人将被蚂蚁吃掉……梅尔加德斯并没有按照人们一般采用的时间顺序来排列事件,而是把整整一个世纪里每一天的事情集中在一起,让它们同时存在于一瞬间。

在小说的结尾部分,奥雷良诺第二破译了羊皮纸手稿并且发现时间的顺序被打乱了,马贡多整部历史中的事件在瞬刻间同时发生了。尽管加西亚·马尔克斯基本上按照时间的先后顺序来创作小说,但是这种时间重叠的暗示在小说中随处可见:来自过去的幽灵显现在现在;将来呈现了过去的特征;失眠症使马贡多居民陷入了永久的现在,既非过去亦非将来。换句话说,时间在马贡多总是呈现出奇怪的现象。在最终时刻我们才发现:在马贡多有两种时间,一种是线性发展的时间,另一种是轮回式发展的时间。这两种时间总是在同一时刻交织在一起。尽管布恩地亚家族沿

ways existed simultaneously, and, even as the Buendías move forward along the straight line of time, they are also returning to the beginning of time in an ever-shrinking spiral.

> 5. *[Aureliano (II)] had already understood that he would never leave that room, for it was foreseen that the city of mirrors (or mirages) would be wiped out by the wind and exiled from the memory of men at the precise moment when Aureliano Babilonia would finish deciphering the parchments, and that everything written on them was unrepeatable since time immemorial and forever more, because races condemned to one hundred years of solitude did not have a second opportunity on earth.*

As he reads Melquíades' writings in the final pages of the novel, Aureliano (II) knows that he will never leave because the destruction of his family is foretold in the prophecies; he believes absolutely in the fate that those prophecies describe. This reference to fate has caused a number of critics to think of *One Hundred Years of Solitude* as a pessimistic book because it seems to say that man has no free will and that all actions are predetermined.

The description of Macondo as a city of "mirrors (or mirages)" also provides a great deal of food for thought. In the final, prophetic scene, mirrors have already been mentioned once, when Aureliano reads about himself reading about himself and feels "as if he were looking into a speaking mirror." A "city of mirrors," then, is a city in which everything is reflected in writing. The written reflection of Macondo exists not only in the prophecies, but also in *One Hundred Years of*

着时间的直线向前发展，但是他们还是会在不断萎缩的轮回中返回到时间的起点。

> 5.［奥雷良诺第二］明白了自己已经不能跨出房间一步了，因为按照羊皮纸手稿的预言，就在奥雷良诺·巴比洛尼亚破译完羊皮纸手稿的最后一瞬间，马贡多这镜子似的（或者海市蜃楼似的）城镇，将被飓风从地面上一扫而光，从人们的记忆中彻底抹掉，羊皮手稿所记载的一切将永远不会重现，遭受百年孤独的家族，注定不会在大地上第二次出现了。

在小说的结尾，当奥雷良诺第二阅读梅尔加德斯的手稿之时，他知道他将无法离开这里，因为预言已经预示家族的毁灭是不可避免的。他完全相信了这些预言所描述的命运。这种命运观使许多批评家认为《百年孤独》是一部悲观小说，因为它似乎在宣告人类没有精神自由，人类的所有的行为都是命中注定的事情。

马贡多被描述为一个"镜子似的（或者海市蜃楼似的）"城镇，这个比喻同样给我们带来了大量可供思考的素材。在最后预言性的场景里，镜子已经被提到过一次了，奥雷良诺第二发现他正在阅读他正在阅读的行为，"就像他望着一面会讲话的镜子似的。"那么，一个"镜子似的"城市就相当于把万事都折射到了小说中的城市。折射马贡多的作品不仅存在于预言当中，而且还存在《百年孤独》小说本身当中。通过联想镜子和海市蜃楼这些虚构的映像，加西亚·马尔克斯

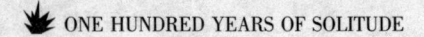

Solitude itself. By coupling mirrors with mirages, which are fictional images, García Márquez invites us to question the reality of Macondo and forces us to be aware of our own act of reading and imagining the story of the town.

This emphasis on reading and interpretation is also very important to this passage. Aureliano has just learned his father's name and refers to himself for the first time as "Aureliano Babilonia." The reference to the tower of Babel emphasizes language and Aureliano's role as a translator and interpreter of the prophecies. García Márquez attaches supernatural power to the act of interpreting a story, and he makes reading an action capable of destroying a town and erasing memory. In doing so, he asks us, as readers, to be aware of the power of interpretation and also to understand that the creation and destruction of Macondo have been entirely created by our own act of reading.

邀请我们质疑马贡多的现实性,迫使我们意识到我们自己的阅读行为的影响,并想象小镇将会发生什么样的故事。

对于这段引文来说,强调阅读和破译也是非常重要的。奥雷良诺第二刚刚获悉自己父亲的名字,他便第一次把自己称作"奥雷良诺·巴比洛尼亚"。提到圣经中的巴别塔是为了强调语言的作用以及奥雷良诺第二作为一个翻译者和破解者在小说中所起到的作用。加西亚·马尔克斯给诠释故事的行为赋予了一种超自然的力量。他认为阅读的行为能够产生一种威力,这种威力足可以毁灭一座小镇,并且将它从人们的记忆中抹掉。作者加西亚·马尔克斯这样做的目的不仅是为了让读者认识到破译力量的威力,而且还让我们了解这样一个事实:马贡多的生存和死亡完全掌控在我们自己的阅读行为之下。

KEY FACTS

Full title
Cien Años de Soledad; One Hundred Years of Solitude

Author
Gabriel García Márquez

Type of work
Novel

Genre
Magical realism

Language
Spanish

Time and place written
1965-1967, Mexico City

Date of first publication
1967

Publisher
Editorial Sudamericanos, S.A.

作品档案

➡ **全名**
《百年孤独》

➡ **作者**
加夫列尔·加西亚·马尔克斯

➡ **作品类型**
长篇小说

➡ **流派**
魔幻现实主义

➡ **语言**
西班牙语

➡ **写作时间和地点**
1965 年～1967 年,墨西哥城

➡ **初版日期**
1967 年

➡ **出版者**
Editorial Sudamericanos, S.A.

Narrator
Omniscient and anonymous, but primarily concerned with what the Buendías are doing and how they are feeling.

Point of view
Third person, but sometimes uses vivid descriptions to show the reader the world through the eyes of one of the characters.

Tone
Although García Márquez writes with wonder and is truly sympathetic to the deep emotions of his characters, he also maintains a certain detachment, so that we are always aware that the book is an account of Macondo as it appears to a modern, cultured eye.

Tense
Past, with occasional flashbacks. There are also brief, single-sentence references to future events that unfold with the novel.

Setting (time)
The early 1800s until the mid 1900s.

Setting (place)
Macondo, a fictional village in Colombia.

Protagonist
The Buendía family; in a single character, Ursula Iguarán,

➡ 叙述者
全知和匿名，但是主要叙述布恩地亚家族在干什么以及他们的感受。

➡ 视角
第三人称视角，但有时通过其中一个人物角色的视角，运用生动的描写给读者展示一个世界。

➡ 语气
尽管加西亚·马尔克斯运用了奇异手法来进行小说的创作并且对他笔下人物角色的深厚情感抱有真挚的同情，但是他还是保持了一定的公正性。因此我们总是能明了这是一部在现代的、有教养人眼中的马贡多小镇的发展史。

➡ 时态
过去时态，偶尔带有闪回。有一些简洁的、单结构句子涉及到了在小说中将来才会发生的事件。

➡ 背景（时间）
19世纪早期至20世纪中期

➡ 背景（地点）
马贡多，位于哥伦比亚的一个虚构的小镇

➡ 主人公
布恩地亚家族；单个角色：乌苏拉·伊瓜兰，她是家

the soul and backbone of the family.

Major conflict
The struggle between old and new ways of life; tradition and modernity.

Rising action
Macondo's civil war; Macondo acquires a banana plantation.

Climax
The banana workers go on strike and are massacred near the train station.

Falling action
The banana plantation shuts down; Macondo returns to its former isolation and backwardness; the Buendía clan dies out; Aureliano (II), who finally discovers how to read Melquíades's prophecies, realizes that the rise and fall of the Buendías has always been destined to happen.

Themes
The subjectivity of experienced reality; the inseparability of past, present, and future; the power of reading and of language.

Motifs
Memory and forgetfulness; the Bible; the gypsies

➡ 族中的灵魂和支柱性人物。

➡ **主要冲突**
新与旧的生活方式之间的斗争；传统与现代之间的斗争

➡ **起势情节**
马贡多的内战；马贡多获得一个香蕉种植园

➡ **高潮**
香蕉工人举行罢工并在铁路附近被屠杀。

➡ **收势情节**
香蕉种植园关闭了；马贡多恢复以前与世隔绝的状态并且衰败了；布恩地亚家族的毁灭；奥雷良诺第二最后终于发现了破解梅尔加德斯预言的秘密并且意识到布恩地亚家族的崛起和毁灭是命中早已注定的事情。

➡ **主题**
经历现实的主观性；过去、现在和未来的不可分割性；阅读和语言的力量

➡ **主题成分**
记忆和健忘；圣经；吉普赛人

Symbols

Little gold fishes; the railroad; the English encyclopedia; the golden chamber pot

Foreshadowing

The fact that both Colonel Aureliano Buendía and Arcadio will face firing squads is heavily foreshadowed in several places. The final, apocalyptic reading of the prophecies is also foreshadowed throughout the novel: García Márquez often mentions the prophecies in passing, and we see various members of the family puzzled by them at different times.

象征

小金鱼;铁路;大英百科全书;金便盆

预示

奥雷良诺·布恩地亚上校和阿卡迪奥都将面对行刑队的事实在好几个地方都被着重预示。在小说的结尾,阅读预言的启示性同样在小说中被预示:加西亚·马尔克斯经常附带地提到预言,而且我们看到家族的不同成员在不同时刻总是被预言所迷惑。

STUDY QUESTIONS & ESSAY TOPICS

Study Questions

1. How might one argue that *One Hundred Years of Solitude* is a realistic novel, despite its fantastic and magical elements?

One Hundred Years of Solitude shares many formal elements with traditional realist novels. García Márquez's novel does not shy away from depictions of violence and sex; it is concerned with, and directly addresses, complex political and social issues. The overall tone of the novel is matter-of-fact, with events portrayed bluntly, as if they actually occurred.

Even those elements in *One Hundred Years of Solitude* that seem "magical" or fantastic are representations of García Márquez's reality. García Márquez's novel describes the unique reality of a Latin America caught between modernity and pre-industrialism, torn by civil war, and ravaged by imperialism. In this environment, what might otherwise seem incredible begins to seem commonplace both to the novelist and to his readers. García Márquez's hometown witnessed a massacre much like the massacre of the workers in Macondo. In García Márquez's Latin America, real life, in its horror and beauty, begins to seem like a fantasy at once horrible and beautiful, and García Márquez's novel is an attempt to recreate and to capture that sense of real life. This is also a

问题·论题

问·答

1.《百年孤独》小说中含有幻想和魔幻的成分,如何来证明它是一部现实主义小说?

《百年孤独》小说借鉴了传统现实主义小说的许多典型成分。加西亚·马尔克斯的小说并没有回避暴力和性的描写;小说的主题往往涉及甚至是直指复杂的政治和社会话题。小说总体的语气是切合实际的,事件的描写采用了平铺直叙的方法,就好像事件实在地发生过。

即使是小说中采用的魔幻或者幻想,也是作者用来描述现实的表现手法。他的小说刻画了这样一个独特的现实:一个处于现代化与前工业化时期夹缝之中的拉丁美洲,它不仅遭受了内战的涂炭,而且还受到了殖民主义的蹂躏。在这种历史背景下,对于作家和读者来说,无论发生如何令人惊叹的事件也都不足为奇。加西亚·马尔克斯的家乡见证了一场大屠杀事件,这场大屠杀事件与小说中马贡多小镇的工人大屠杀事件非常相似。在加西亚·马尔克斯的眼里,拉丁美洲原有的幽默和美好的真实生活演变成了一种幻想,这种幻想在即刻间使人感到既恐怖又美丽,而加西亚·马尔克斯的小说试图再现并且捕捉那种真实生活的感觉。这同样是一部创造神话的小说,既汲取了圣经

novel that grants myth—both biblical and indigenous Latin American--the same level of credibility as fact. It is sensitive to the magic that superstition and religion infuse into the world. *One Hundred Years of Solitude*, then, is a realistic novel in the sense that it asserts a unity between the surreal and the real: it asserts that magic is as real—as relevant, as present and as powerful—as what we normally take to be reality.

2. What is the attitude of *One Hundred Years of Solitude* toward modernity? What is its attitude toward tradition?

Modern technology and culture, along with the capitalism associated with them, often destabilize Macondo: the arrival of the train reduces the town to chaos, and the banana company is one of the few true forces of evil in the novel. Tradition in *One Hundred Years of Solitude* is a source of comfort and wisdom and a source of the novel's formal inspiration, as well: *One Hundred Years of Solitude* owes a great deal to the indigenous Latin American folkloric and mythological traditions. But the division between tradition and modernity is not quite so simple. For instance, the moral codes adopted by the novel's most respected characters are not traditional codes but are, instead, far more progressive. Aureliano Segundo, for instance, is rewarded for his extra-marital affair with Petra Cotes. Traditional Catholicism is seen as repressive, while the novel's own version of modern moral codes prevails.

故事的典故又吸收了拉美国家本土神话的元素,神话的可信度达到了与现实接近的程度。迷信和宗教融入现实激发了魔幻的敏感性。《百年孤独》小说肯定了超现实与现实之间的统一性:就像我们正常对现实采取的看法一样,《百年孤独》小说断定魔幻可以被看作是现实的、与现实相关的、存在于当下的以及具有现实影响力的。那么,从这个意义上说,《百年孤独》小说是一部现实主义小说。

2.《百年孤独》小说对现代化以及传统价值观分别持有何种态度?

现代化技术和现代文化以及与之相联系的资本主义制度总是给马贡多带来动荡和不安。火车的到来使马贡多陷入了混乱,香蕉公司更是为数不多的罪恶之源之一。《百年孤独》小说中的传统价值观是快乐和智慧的源泉,也是小说创作灵感的源头:《百年孤独》小说的成功主要得益于它汲取了拉美国家本土的民间传说以及传统的神话故事。然而,划清传统和现代之间的界限并非这么容易。例如,小说中最令人欣赏的角色所持有的道德标准并非传统的道德标准,反而更具反叛性。比如奥雷良诺·塞贡多与佩特娜·柯特的婚外恋情反而得到了奖赏。传统的天主教教义被视为是压抑人性的,而小说本身所提倡的现代道德标准却占了上风。

3. The famous critic Harold Bloom calls *One Hundred Years of Solitude* "The Bible of Macondo." To what extent is this true? To what extent does One Hundred Years of Solitude pattern itself after—or diverge from—the Bible?

First of all, certain elements of *One Hundred Years of Solitude*'s plot are extremely similar to that of the Bible. The novel opens with two characters in an uncivilized area of the world, a world so new that many things still have no names. The characters, like Adam and Eve, establish a progeny that both populates the world and experiences the world's gradual departure from a state of pristine beauty devoid of pain or death. When the heinous massacre occurs, in which three thousand people are killed, it rains for five years, cleansing the Earth in water in much the same way that the biblical flood in the time of Noah did. Finally, the book ends with an irreversible, apocalyptic destruction.

But beyond elements of the plot, stylistic qualities of the novel make the book function in a way similar to the Bible. Not only has the entire course of events been prophesied by Melquíades, but at the end of the book, the distinction between Melquíades' prophesy and the actual text, *One Hundred Years of Solitude* which we are reading, is blurred. It is possible, then, that the novel is itself, like the Bible, a book of prophesy. But the prophesies do not necessarily function for the residents of Macondo as the Bible does for those who read it. If the book is indeed identical with Melquíades' prophesies, because the prophesies are written in Sanskrit, those who inhabit Macondo cannot turn to them for guidance or information about the future. While the Bible has a long tradition of exe-

3. 著名的批评家哈罗德·布鲁姆把《百年孤独》小说称为：一部"马贡多的圣经。"你认为这种观点对吗？《百年孤独》在多大程度上仿效或者解构了圣经？

首先，《百年孤独》情节中的许多成分与圣经极为相似。小说以两个角色处在一个未经开化的世界为开端，这块天地还是新开辟的，许多东西都叫不出名字。这两个角色，就像亚当和夏娃，繁衍了后代。后代们开始生活在这个世界里并且体验这个世界逐渐地从一种纯真、没有痛苦和死亡的状态中脱离出来。当令人发指的大屠杀发生之后，在这场屠杀中有3000多人遇害，天上的雨下了五年之久，雨水净化了土地，就如同圣经故事中诺亚时期的洪水起到了净化罪恶的作用一样。最后，小说以一个不可避免的启示性的毁灭作为结尾。

然而除了小说情节成分发挥的作用之外，小说的体裁在风格上也类似于圣经。事件发生的整个过程不仅被梅尔加德斯所预言，而且在小说的结尾，梅尔加德斯的预言与我们正在阅读的小说文本之间的界限被弄得模糊不清。《百年孤独》小说本身，像圣经一样，有可能就是一部预言。但是这部预言并不能为马贡多的居民起到任何作用，不像圣经那样能为阅读它的人提供他们想要的东西。《百年孤独》小说事实上与梅尔加德斯的预言相似，因为预言是用梵语写成的，住在马贡多的居民无法借助于它去引导自己或者预知未来。圣经具有注释和解释的永久传统，而《百年孤独》所具备的这种功能仅限于奥雷良诺第二以及我们读

gesis and interpretation, *One Hundred Years of Solitude* is available only to Aureliano, who finally deciphers it, and to us, the readers. As a result, when compared to the prophesies of the Bible, the novel's prophesies are silent and inaccessible to those who could most use them.

Suggested Essay Topics

1. In what ways can *One Hundred Years of Solitude* be seen as a fable about the history of human civilization?

2. How does García Márquez use symbolism in *One Hundred Years of Solitude*? To what extent does the novel function as a network of symbols, allegories, and parables; to what extent can it stand on its own as a narrative?

3. *One Hundred Years of Solitude* is a vastly ambitious book, attempting to bridge many dualisms and appeal to many audiences: it is both general and particular, both realistic and magical. Is the book successful in its attempts to encompass such a vast scope of experiences and voices? What are the narrative shortcomings of One Hundred Years of Solitude?

4. With which character in *One Hundred Years of Solitude* do you most identify? Why? Is there any character in the novel who is wholly admirable, anyone who is wholly evil?

者。作为结果，与圣经的预言相比，对于那些最想使用它们的人来说，小说的预言是沉默无声的、难以接近的。

推荐论题

1. 《百年孤独》小说是否可以被看作是一部有关人类文明历史的寓言？

2. 加西亚·马尔克斯在《百年孤独》小说中是怎么使用象征手法的？小说在多大程度上起到了一个象征、寓言以及比喻的综合作用的？小说本身是一部完整的故事吗？

3. 《百年孤独》小说是一部宏篇巨著，吸引了众多的读者。小说试图调和诸多的二元矛盾，比如一般与特殊；现实与魔幻。小说试图折射广泛领域中的社会现实以及话语权，从这方面来说，《百年孤独》是否在这方面获得了成功？《百年孤独》小说的叙述缺点是什么？

4. 你对《百年孤独》小说中的哪一个角色的印象最为深刻？为什么？小说中有没有你最欣赏的角色？或者有没有最令你憎恶的角色？

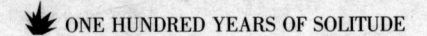

5. What do you think is the novel's understanding of human nature? Is it a fundamentally optimistic novel? To what extent does García Márquez believe that love is possible?

6. To what extent is the novel's title, *One Hundred Years of Solitude*, an important commentary on the narrative in the book? What connections does the book make between knowledge and solitude? Is solitude an unavoidable condition of human nature?

7. To what extent do you think that *One Hundred Years of Solitude* is a novel particularly concerned with Latin American culture and politics? To what extent is it a novel designed to appeal broadly to all readers?

5. 你对小说所理解的人性是如何看待的?《百年孤独》从根本上说是一部乐观小说吗？作者加西亚·马尔克斯在多大程度上相信爱是真实的?

6. 作为小说的书名——《百年孤独》能概括小说的主题吗？小说如何处理知识和孤独之间的关系的？孤独是人性当中不可避免的归宿吗？

7. 你认为《百年孤独》小说与拉美文化和政治之间有多大程度的联系?《百年孤独》小说是一部为迎合大众口味而创作的普世小说吗？

REVIEW & RESOURCES

回味・深入

Quiz 四选一

1. What is the name of the gypsy who brings the magnet and telescope to Macondo?

(A) Alfonso

(B) Riohacha

(C) Melquíades

(D) Teófilo Vargas

2. What is the nickname of the woman who beats Aureliano Segundo in an eating contest?

(A) Remedios

(B) The Elephant

(C) Petra Cotes

(D) Lourdes

3. When Colonel Aureliano Buendía retires from the war, what does he spend his time making?

(A) Golden fishes

(B) Ceramic pottery

(C) Lottery tickets

(D) Maps

4. What is the name of the man whom José Arcadio Buendía kills for making fun of him?

(A) Giovanni della Mirandola

(B) Mario Vargas Llosa

(C) El Guapo

(D) Prudencio Aguilar

5. After a certain point in the novel, what mark distinguishes Colonel Aureliano Buendía's seventeen sons?

(A) They are all extremely fat

(B) They all have golden eyes

(C) They all have crosses on their forehead

(D) They all wear only black clothing

6. What invention does Aureliano Triste bring to Macondo?

(A) The railroad

(B) The gyroscope

(C) The airplane

(D) Gunpowder

7. The civil war is fought between which two parties?

(A) The monarchists and the loyalists

(B) The Liberals and the Conservatives

(C) The Extremists and the Pacifists

(D) The Whigs and the Tories

8. According to Buendía family tradition, what will happen to babies born of incestuous relationships?

(A) They will be extremely small

- (B) They will float away into the sky
- (C) They will have wings like bats
- (D) They will have tails like pigs

9. What happens to Remedios the Beauty?
- (A) She is abducted by gypsies
- (B) She floats away into the sky
- (C) She marries the local bookseller
- (D) She becomes a hermit

10. How does the government put Arcadio to death?
- (A) Firing squad
- (B) Hanging
- (C) Electrocution
- (D) Beheading

11. Aureliano (II) discovers that the prophecies are written in which language?
- (A) Latin
- (B) Hittite
- (C) Ancient Greek
- (D) Sanskrit

12. Which of the following best describes Dr. Alirio Noguera?
- (A) Pediatrician
- (B) Liberal radical
- (C) Alchemist
- (D) Fortune teller

13. Where is Ursula Iguarán's gold hidden?

(A) Under her bed

(B) In the church

(C) Underneath the tree in the backyard

(D) In Colonel Aureliano Buendía's workshop

14. What job does Mauricio Babilonia do for the banana company?

(A) He is a foreman

(B) He is a security guard

(C) He is a mechanic

(D) He is a banana picker

15. What instrument does Pietro Crespi bring to the Buendía household?

(A) The harp

(B) The pianola

(C) The harpsichord

(D) The timpani

16. What is the name of the first magistrate to come to Macondo, whose daughter marries Colonel Aureliano Buendía?

(A) Don Apolinar Moscote

(B) Don Pedro Vasquez

(C) Don Reymondo Ordo?ez

(D) Don Isaac Abravanel

17. As a mark of her regret, what does Amaranta wear until she dies?

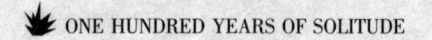

(A) A cross around her neck
(B) A scarlet handkerchief over her hair
(C) A black bandage on her hand
(D) A crown of thorns around her forehead

18. Which bad habit does Rebeca not have when she first comes to Macondo?
(A) Eating dirt
(B) Eating whitewash
(C) Sucking her finger
(D) Bathing in mud

19. What is the name of the black woman who becomes Aureliano (II)'s lover?
(A) Nigromanta
(B) Cornelia
(C) Claudia Arribata
(D) Marcela

20. Gaston, Amaranta Ursula's husband, tries to start which kind of business?
(A) Selling books
(B) Delivering airmail
(C) Teaching music
(D) Making ice

21. Jose Aureliano Segundo is the sole surviving witness to what catastrophe?
(A) The flood in town
(B) The great fire in the church

(C) The collapse of the Buendía house in an earthquake

(D) The massacre of the striking workers

22. How do Aureliano Segundo and Petra Cotes become rich?

(A) They find úrsula Iguarán's buried gold

(B) Their farm animals breed extremely rapidly

(C) They are very successful selling the candy that they make

(D) They go to work at the banana plantation

23. Aureliano José is shot in the back while running away from soldiers in which building?

(A) The movie theater

(B) The church

(C) The brothel

(D) The Buendía house

24. What infectious disease does Rebeca bring to Macondo?

(A) Measles

(B) Insomnia

(C) Leprosy

(D) Smallpox

25. What do Aureliano (II) and Amaranta Ursula name their baby?

(A) Aureliano

(B) Mauricio Babilonia

(C) José

(D) Gerineldo Marquez

Suggestions for Further Reading
相关链接

BELL, MICHAEL. *Gabriel García Márquez: Solitude and Solidarity*. United Kingdom: Macmillan, 1993.

BLOOM, HAROLD, ed. *Modern Critical Views: Gabriel García Márquez*. New York: Chelsea House Publishers, 1989.

"Gabriel García Márquez." From the Internet Public Library.

GARCÍA MÁRQUEZ, GABRIEL. *One Hundred Years of Solitude*. Trans. Gregory Rabassa. New York: Harper & Row, 1970.

JANES, REGINA. ONE HUNDRED YEARS OF SOLITUDE: *Modes of Reading*. Boston: Twayne Publishers, 1991.

MCGUIRK, BERNARD AND RICHARD CARDWELL, eds. *Gabriel García Márquez: New Readings*. New York: Cambridge University Press, 1987.

MCMURRAY, GEORGE R., ed. *Critical Essays on Gabriel García Márquez*. Boston: G.K. Hall, 1987.

Answer Key:
1.C 2.B 3.A 4.D 5.C 6.A 7. 8.D 9.B 10.A 11.D 12.B 13.A 14.C 15.B 16.A 17.C 18.D 19.A 20.B 21.D 22.B 23.A 24.B 25.A

哈佛蓝星双语名著导读(50 册)
Today's Most Popular Study Guides

汤姆·索亚历险记 ((The Adventures of Tom Sawyer)
哈克贝利·芬历险记 (The Adventures of Huckleberry Finn)
西线无战事 (All Quiet on the Western Front)
哈利·波特与魔法石 (Harry Potter and the Sorcerer's Stone)
觉醒 (The Awakening)

宠儿 (Beloved)
最蓝的眼睛 (The Bluest Eye)
美丽新世界 (Brave New World)
野性的呼唤 (The Call of the Wild)
麦田守望者 (The Catcher in the Rye)

第二十二条军规 (Catch-22)
炼狱 (The Crucible)
推销员之死 (Death of a Salesman)
华氏451度 (Fahrenheit 451)
永别了,武器 (A Farewell to Arms)

弗兰肯斯坦 (Frankenstein)
愤怒的葡萄 (The Grapes of Wrath)
了不起的盖茨比 (The Great Gatsby)
飘 (Gone with the Wind)
黑暗的中心 (Heart of Darkness)

广岛 (Hiroshima)
土生子 (Native Son)
隐形人 (Invisible Man)
简·爱 (Jane Eyre)
喜福会 (The Joy Luck Club)

珍珠 （The Pearl）
屠场 （The Jungle）
雾都孤儿 （Oliver Twist）
蝇王 （Lord of the Flies）
一个青年艺术家的画像 （A Portrait of the Artist as a Young Man）

鲁滨孙飘流记 （Robinson Crusoe）
白鲸 （Moby-Dick）
喧哗与骚动 （The Sound and the Fury）
苔丝 （Tess of the d'Urbervilles）
人与鼠 （Of Mice and Men）

老人与海 （The Old Man and the Sea）
金银岛 （Treasure Island）
傲慢与偏见 （Pride and Prejudice）
红色英勇勋章 （The Red Badge of Courage）
太阳依旧升起 （The Sun Also Rises）

一个人的和平 （A Separate Peace）
红字 （The Scarlet Letter）
双城记 （A Tale of Two Cities）
欲望号街车 （A Streetcar Named Desire）
他们的眼睛望着上帝 （Their Eyes Were Watching God）

瓦解 （Things Fall Apart）
杀死一只知更鸟 （To Kill a Mockinghird）
汤姆叔叔的小屋 （Uncle Tom's Cabin）
远大前程 （Great Expectation）
呼啸山庄 （Wuthering Heights）

哈佛蓝星双语名著导读(新 28 册)
Today's Most Popular Study Guides

安琪拉的灰烬 (Angela's Ashes)
冷山 (Cold Mountain)
浮士德博士 (Doctor Faustus)
堂吉诃德 (Don Quixote)
艰难时世 (Hard Times)

小妇人 (Little Women)
失乐园 (Paradise Lost)
坎特伯雷故事集 (The Canterbury Tales)
局外人 (The Stranger)
尤利西斯 (Ulysses)

瓦尔登湖 (Walden)
玩偶之家 (A Doll's House)
印度之行 (A Passage to India)
安娜·卡列尼娜 (Anna Karenina)
黑孩子 (Black Boy)

罪与罚 (Crime and Punishment)
都柏林人 (Dubliners)
爱玛 (Emma)
丧钟为谁而鸣 (For Whom the Bell Tolls)
格列佛游记 (Gulliver's Travels)

悲惨世界 (Les Misérables)
包法利夫人 (Madam Bovary)
百年孤独 (One Hundred Years of Solitude)
所罗门之歌 (Song of Solomon)

基督山伯爵 (The Count of Monte Cristo)
魔戒前传: 霍比特人 (The Hobbit)
卡斯特桥市长 (The Mayor of Casterbridge)
战争与和平 (War and Peace)